A YEAR IN INK

VOLUME 9

SAN DIEGO WRITERS, INK

A YEAR IN INK

ANTHOLOGY VOLUME 9

Edited by Bonnie ZoBell
and Sydney Brown

THE INK SPOT PRESS

A Year in Ink, Volume 9 is a publication of

The Ink Spot Press
San Diego Writers, Ink
NTC at Liberty Station
2730 Historic Decatur Road
Barracks 16, Suite 202
San Diego, CA 92106

Many thanks go to Arin Winkler, Kristen Fogle, Kim Keeline, our first readers, editors, and hardworking proofreaders.

Cover image by Jenny Siegwart
www.jennysiegwart.com

Cover and layout design:
Arin Winkler
www.WinklerDesigns.com

ISBN: 978-0-9799204-8-6

Printed in the United States of America
Printed by Lightning Source, Inc.

CONTENTS

PROSE EDITOR'S NOTES

BONNIE ZOBELL

When I finished my BA in English at SDSU many years ago, there was little to nothing going on in San Diego for writers, not to mention the lack of MFA programs on campuses. One of my professors suggested I look up MFAs in the library, and so I did. Needless to say, this was pre-computer. I spent hours in the library, fascinated by all the places I could go out of state. I wasn't very happy at the time, I needed some distance from my family, and I wasn't very good at anything besides writing. I applied to fifteen programs, my mind bustling with the possibilities of all the literary places I could go and do nothing but write, where other people lived and breathed literary dreams, talked about books instead of remodeling, wrote as often as they paid bills and grocery shopped. I moved to New York City.

Thirty-five years later I feel so excited to get to judge work for the San Diego Writers, Ink anthology, *A Year in Ink, Vol. 9* from so many talented San Diego writers! Now we have San Diego Writers, Ink, Vermin on the Mount, So Say We All, AuthorPreneurs, MFAs offered at a flock of universities and colleges, writing conferences, and a bunch of other writing-centric groups and organizations.

Most importantly, what a feast of diverse work I got to read for the anthology. What a dazzling group of writers our city now has living here. How lucky we are. Such disparate styles and themes and intentions. We are urban in the best sense of the word and embrace such an assortment of individual thinking. Gone are the days when we could be known only as the land of military bases and a retirement community. The pieces selected for this anthology are as divergent as Deng/Bernstein's "Boy Who Fell Through Time," the curious tale of a boy growing up in the Sudan whose father fights a lion, and the two chapters from Laurie Richard's novel *Barren Branches,* about a family with a drama unfolding while they are seemingly stuck in a place so barren and cold in our own Midwest that you need to wrap yourself in a blanket to read them.

Which brings to mind the hardest part of my job: How in the world do you choose between such wonderfully distinct pieces of writings? None of them are seeking to do the same thing. So many are beautiful in completely different ways. There's Leslie Ferguson's chapters from her book *Schizophrenia's Daughter: Based on a True Story,* a harrowing tale of a mentally ill mother who runs off with her children she's not supposed to have; then there's Amy Nastase's piece about a boy in China who's the only one in his apartment building who speaks English and has to take and translate a phone call from America and then tell his neighbors disturbing news about their son. In David J. Schmidt's funny flash, "Deus Ex Machina," Lucifer and God submit a manuscript for publication.

With all the talk these days of editors needing to be more open to voices different from their own, I tried very hard to really *hear* assorted tones, cultures, sexes, ages, and so on. Reading anonymously, though, I could only pick what I liked, and I ended up picking more female writers than male. I don't know what that means. I don't know what the statistics were for all the writing that was sent in. It's good that San Diego Writers, Ink chooses different editors for the anthology every year. And despite all that, what a pleasure all the submissions were to read.

San Diego is a great place for writing.

POETRY EDITOR'S NOTES

SYDNEY BROWN

The dazzling poems in this volume of *A Year in Ink* display a rich diversity in content and form. While it is not possible to address every poem I have selected for this year's anthology, I can attest to the fact that I am equally delighted and haunted by the ways in which the writers use the page to explore the internal and external landscapes of experience. I will even go so far as to say that these poems give their readers a new way to be in the world. San Diego writers are not afraid to take risks; don't let anyone tell you differently.

The reader does not have to travel far to experience what I describe. The first two poems, Marg Wafer's "In the Desert Alone" and Allen Fraser Clark's "Quicksilver," represent this pioneering spirit in content and form. The collection opens with a writer "In the desert alone." In a sprawling city envied for fun and sun, we meet a woman who is drawn to something that frightens her: "silence." While she is able to master what she needs to do to survive in the desert alone, to "count her victories," one is left wondering where she is with regards to the self in this landscape, if she is indeed able to come "clean" of her daily, and perhaps existential, anxieties. Wafer chooses to leave her ending open, open for the casual reader to count the speaker's accomplishments with her; however, the close reader will not settle on "clean" and travel back into the poem to ponder his or her own fears and the ways in which we do and do not confront them.

Existential fear is not at the core of Clark's "Quicksilver," as his poem uses language to express delight in the writer's ability to reshape the physical world. We move from one poet's dark curtain of night to a second poet's celebration of morning; however, it is a morning that does not cooperate with the speaker's desire for sun-filled living, as we discover "the morning's rub" / "A sky like mud." Clark's phrasing is whimsical, but his complaint is clear: he craves the "smack of blue light," the sun to which he has grown accustomed. Nevertheless, with gusto the poet triumphs over his conflict. What the natural world does not offer, he creates in language, thus giving the reader "an afternoon with a front-row bullring seat," replete with *"sombra y sol."* And he does not stop there. Like Whitman sounding his "barbaric yawp," Clark bangs his "bright drum"—the desire to be "wild and reckless, even risk samsaric breach" in his passion for language and life. While the first poem in his collection asks the reader to contemplate their existence, Clark's poem encourages us to seize the day and turn the page.

While each poem in this collection deserves the time I have given these two, I encourage you to travel alone. Lose yourself in pages where poets reconstruct sensual and linguistic landscapes, ranging from one's own backyard to an abandoned home, from the streets of Rome and India to a "barren Utah prairie" and a "little corner of Texas," to the weather of kindness, an homage to E.E. Cummings' linguistic carnival. Line by line, human and creature connections—in all their messy and beautiful orchestrations—are dragged outside, saved from drowning, secretly indulged. Silence is traversed. The pistachio, Georgia O'Keefe, Marcel Duchamp, and something as seemingly simple as paper, are newly praised. Hunters, a mother, and a sister's lover are indicted, and a father's literary legacy turns his daughter's stone heart into a "golden and glowing fruit-ripe ball of love." The words "high yella heifa" and "darkies" hurt a child, but when a teacher speaks the child's true name in "the way your mouth feels after the first bite of sweet potato pie—warm, creamy," we are all soothed. A request as straightforward as "Lávese Las Manos" unfurls into an exhilarating tribute to hands, "the little biscuit fist / that some day may pitch a baseball" and "stop the index pointed on the trigger." And finally, the perimeter of a familiar pasture ("perimeter"—such a carefully selected word) is walked by two. However, like the lesson we learn pages earlier from the wolf who loves an elephant "more than meat," the poem "Old Friends" offers its companion-reader a new way to be in the world, a place where love that comes naturally can be untimely and consequently, unspoken, so to leave one "must break / spider silk shimmying / between the gateposts." There is remarkable wisdom and restraint in the way these lines embody the complexity of choice, love, and the passing of time.

Welcome to the ninth volume of *A Year in Ink,* an astonishing testament to the creative catalyst San Diego Writers, Ink is, and always has been, to our diverse literary community.

SAN DIEGO WRITERS, INK

A YEAR
IN INK

ANTHOLOGY VOLUME 9

IN THE DESERT ALONE

MARG WAFER

One fiery tip on an ocotillo bush in mid-May,
most of the reds gone for the summer.
Away from the duties of work, home,
but my anxious thoughts have come along
for the ride. Bastards.
I light the stove, boil the water,
drink the tea.

On my hike to a palm oasis,
trickles of water grace the brittle sand.
At camp there is birdsong, the patter of my pen,
traveling across the page.

When night drops its curtain,
there are no stars, no moon.
Wind flirts with my hair, carries insects inside,
the zipper on my tent flap broken.
I burrow into my bag. The wind dies down
and I sleep inside a vast silence.
This is what I came here for, silence,
and it frightens me.

I count my victories in the morning.
Lit the stove, pitched the tent, slept alone,
and worked the camp shower with its
small bag of water and long hose I opened
and closed, came clean.

THE PHONE CALL

AMY NASTASE

"Chen Long, Chen Long! Xing lai, wake up," his mother called as she opened his bedroom door.

Chen Long rolled over to see his mother entering his room. Through the light coming into his dark room from the hallway, Chen Long could see her frantically waving her hand. He squinted at the neon-lit numbers on the alarm clock. 4:10 a.m. Although he couldn't make out her face, this was far enough out of the ordinary for Chen Long to know that something was amiss.

His mother regularly preached the importance of sleep, citing not very scientifically proven advice she had read online about creating the perfect sleep environment to boost scholarly learning when his father grumbled that the TV was being turned off the minute after Chen Long went to sleep each night. Chen Long could sympathize with his father in this regard. His mother wouldn't allow the TV to be on in Chen Long's presence before bedtime because it would disrupt him from his homework and then his father couldn't watch news or sports late at night because the sound might travel down the hallway of their two-bedroom apartment and through Chen Long's closed bedroom door.

"What's the point of even owning a TV?" his father would complain.

"It's for the guests," was his mother's typical reply.

How was he supposed to know what was happening, his father would counter, if he couldn't watch the news.

"Read the newspaper," his mother would always answer, a response that would definitively end the conversation for a day or two before the issue was raised again.

"Chen Long. You are awake? Good. Come quick," his mother said as she approached his bed, holding out his robe.

Chen Long pushed the blanket off and stood up, taking the proffered robe and clumsily fitting his arms into the sleeves. The robe was only three months old, but Chen Long's thirteen-year-old body had almost rendered the sleeves too short already.

"What is going on?" Chen Long finally woke up enough to ask.

"Mrs. Tan has a phone call from America. She needs you to speak English."

The Tans lived across the hallway, also in a two-bedroom apartment, although one bedroom was unoccupied since their son, Zheng, had left to go study engineering in Chicago two years ago.

Zheng was ten years older than Chen Long. His mother liked to remark how young Zheng used to build elaborate block structures in his parents' living room and how he was so well mannered and polite and how she wished for such good fortune on Chen Long's parents when they first moved into the apartment building. They were newlyweds then, waiting for the right time to have their one child. When Chen Long's mother did become pregnant, she spent every day for the next nine months praying to her ancestors for a boy, a boy who could grow up to be just like Zheng. And so Chen Long was given multiple sets of blocks to play with before he could even stack more than two of them on top of each other. Now that he was older, he was encouraged to focus on math and go to after school academies three times a week to improve his English.

"America has the best universities," his mother often remarked. "Harvard, Yale, Stanford. Everyone in the world knows Harvard."

Chen Long followed his mother across the hallway, excited to play the role of the hero, but also nervous because the only Americans he had ever spoken English to were his academy teachers, a series of bubbly young females—Katie, Allison, Mindy, and the latest one, Sarah. Sarah was the prettiest, and as he took the receiver from Mrs. Tan, Chen Long could imagine telling a recounting of this phone call to Sarah in class that afternoon and how she would surely smile and congratulate him on his linguistic success.

"Hello. My name is Chen Long. I speak English," he bravely spoke into the phone.

"Hello?" a man's solid voice answered back. "I'm trying to reach Mr. and Mrs. Tan. This is about their son, Zheng."

Chen Long took a calming breath. He was able

to understand this American man without any problems! In his mind, he snickered a little at the man's mispronunciation of Zheng's name. But this happened all the time at Chen Long's English academy. The students would share stories of their teachers' slip-ups as they walked home. Americans were just not very good at Chinese names.

"This is Mr. and Mrs. Tan's phone. They do not speak English. I am their neighbor."

"Oh, I see. I'm Peter Atler, the Assistant Dean of Graduate Students at the University of Chicago. I'm calling because Zheng..." Mr. Atler paused, thankfully, thought Chen Long. He had gotten a little fast there and Chen Long wasn't sure what Dean meant, but he could just tell the Tans the man was a professor. That would be good enough.

"How old are you, Chen, is it?" Mr. Atler asked.

"I am thirteen years old."

"I see. Ah, are there any adults that speak English there? It would be better if I could talk to one of them."

Chen Long felt his heart becoming indignant. What was wrong with his English? He hadn't made any mistakes so far as he could tell.

"No. Mr. and Mrs. Tan do not speak English. My parents do not speak English. But I take English lessons. I happy to help you."

"Well," Mr. Atler started and then paused again. "I don't want to do this, but Mr. and Mrs. Tan need to know about their son right away." He paused again and then muttered so rapidly that Chen Long could barely follow, "Oh, God. I've never had to do this before. This just isn't right. You're only thirteen."

Chen Long fought his indignation again. The Tans were looking at him expectantly. His father had wandered over by now as well, and both his parents were also staring at him, hopeful that he could prove the value of all his extra English assignments right here in this apartment.

"It is okay," Chen Long assured Mr. Atler, "I can help. I am very dependable." Chen Long smiled—this was a word Sarah had taught his class last week. As always, Chen Long had raised his hand to answer every one of Sarah's questions about the previous day's reading material. Sarah laughed, "Chen Long, you are so dependable! You always do your homework and know the right answer." When she laughed, the corners of her blue eyes wrinkled up and the freckles on her cheeks looked like they were dancing.

"Yes, I'm afraid you will have to do," Mr. Atler replied. "Please tell Mr. and Mrs. Tan that Zheng was in a car accident. He was injured very badly and unfortunately, he did not survive. I am very sorry. Zheng was a good student and a promising engineer. We will miss him very much."

Chen Long gripped the phone as his stomach started to rise up into his chest. In the still room, he was afraid everyone could hear how rapid his heart was now beating. But he didn't want to say anything yet that might frighten the Tans, because surely he must have misheard or misunderstood what the professor had said. Yes, that's probably what happened—after all, it was his first phone call with America.

"Zheng is hurt? He at the hospital?"

"Yes."

"He be okay?"

"No, I'm sorry. His injuries were very severe. The doctors couldn't do anything."

"I do not understand. You are saying, Zheng is died?"

"Yes, I'm afraid Zheng has died. I wish you did not have to be the one to hear this. I'm sure it is a big shock to you, but I need you to please tell the Tans for me."

"Yes. Okay. I can," Chen Long quietly said into the receiver before gently placing it on the table.

Chen Long tried to lift his eyes towards Mr. and Mrs. Tan, but memories of Zheng began flashing in front of him as vivid as if Zheng was actually standing in the room, nonchalantly leaning against the table where Mr. Tan now sat silently observing.

"Chen Long, what is the message? It is not polite to make Mr. and Mrs. Tan wait." His mother's voice broke up the vision of Zheng.

Chen Long swallowed and then dashed over to his mother's side. His most recent growth spurt had put him within an inch of her height, so he found it easy to whisper in her ear, "The man from the university said Zheng is dead. A car accident."

Chen Long was trembling by the time the last three words came out, and as soon as the final syllable left his lips, he sprinted out of the Tans apartment, across the hallway, and into the sanctuary of his bedroom, his mother's gasp and then Mrs. Tan's sudden shriek rising over the slamming of the doors behind him.

Chen Long pulled his Mp3 player out of his backpack and jammed the earbuds into his ears. He hit play immediately, not caring which song was next in the playlist and fumbled with the volume before it reached its highest setting. He flung himself back into bed, pulled the blanket over his head and squeezed his eyes shut.

* * * *

"Chen Long. It is time for school." His father squeezed his shoulder. The Mp3 player was still in his hand and he quickly turned the volume down.

"Chen Long. It is time for school," his father calmly repeated. "Your mother is with Mrs. Tan and I need to go to the office. Wake up and get ready now."

Chen Long slowly emerged from under the blanket. His father was by the front door, slipping on his shoes. Right before he left, he turned back and sighed. "We are proud of you. But there might be more phone calls. Make sure you focus on your studies today."

Chen Long nodded.

"Good," his father replied, and then quietly disappeared into the hallway.

Chen Long quickly dressed and put on his backpack. On the kitchen table was his breakfast of a *baozi* and a thermos of warm soy milk that he grabbed before leaving the empty apartment. In the hallway, he locked the front door as quickly as he could and then ran towards the stairs, taking great care not to look at the Tans' closed door.

There was a small group of neighborhood boys already gathered at the bus stop, shouts and laughter ringing through the air. Normally Chen Long would join them, teasing Jin about his unruly hair and comparing answers to the previous night's math homework with Wei, but today he lingered at the edge of the pack, sipping from his thermos, the *baozi* still wrapped up.

When the city bus lurched up to the stop, the standard jostling occurred as the boys rushed the open doors. Chen Long was the last to board, quietly slipping into an open bench right behind the driver. The other boys, including his friends, were so absorbed in their pre-school rowdiness that they didn't notice when Chen Long impulsively pulled the stopcord two stops before the school and stepped off the bus as the driver furrowed his brow and shook his head before chugging down the street.

Chen Long stood on the bustling sidewalk and watched as a puff of exhaust burst out from the bus's tailpipe before it was swallowed up by the mass of other cars, trucks, and buses clogging the six-lane road. He had seen the store facades in front of him hundreds of times before as the bus ambled past every morning and afternoon, yet he felt like he was a stranger in this part of his own city, having never actually set foot in this stretch of the street before. He peered down the block both ways and then across the intersection, wondering which direction to take. He had never skipped a day of school before, but today was different. He was alive today and Zheng was not.

Chen Long had not known anyone who had died before. All four of his grandparents were alive and frequently stopped by the apartment. Occasionally, they would relay the news of a distant relative's death, but without having met any of them, they were just names, and so Chen Long had to muster up an appropriate look of sorrow on his face for a moment before the conversation continued on to the success of his uncle's business or the rising price of pork.

Down a small side street, Chen Long spied an Internet cafe and set off towards it. The attendant, a college-aged girl with pink streaks in her short hair and a nose ring, didn't say a word as she took his yuan. Only when she handed him the printed slip of paper with his assigned computer and login information, did she even make eye contact. If she noticed his uniform or deduced that at 7:42 on a Tuesday morning, he was clearly skipping school, she gave no reproaching look nor any sign of concern at all.

Sitting down at the computer, Chen Long wondered if his mother was still at the Tans' apartment or if she was on her way to the fitness center for her daily exercise class. Would she whisper the news about the Tans' son to her friends as they sat in the locker room, pulling on their athletic shoes?

Chen Long played his favorite video game for a bit, but after dying three times in seven minutes, he quit. He lightly tapped his fingers on the sticky keyboard before opening up a new browser. He watched clips from the previous day's NBA games and checked Yao Ming's latest stats—14 points, 2 assists, 3 rebounds. Yao was his favorite player. Zheng's too.

Chen Long looked at the time, 8:23. He was restless, but he had to take care not to draw attention to himself or else he would be reported to the truancy office. He did not know that skipping school would be so exhausting. 8:24. He sighed, and then without thinking, typed Zheng's name into a search engine, but in pinyin, rather than characters.

The first result was Zheng's listing on his university's departmental directory. Besides the small picture of his face, was his email and area of research.

A flashing box popped up on the screen. Your session will end in five minutes. He ignored it.

The next result was what he had secretly hoped to find, even though his hand trembled as he clicked on the link. A story from an American newspaper filled the screen, the headline—'Chinese Student Killed in Car Accident.'

He did his best to read it, struggling to remember all the English vocabulary words he had ever memorized, including the ones used a single time, on a test usually, and then discarded from his mind to make room for more. Thankfully, the news report was brief and Chen Long was able to understand that the car accident had happened early Monday morning, Zheng had been the p-a-s-s-e-n-g-e-r, there were two other people named, both called drivers and one of them was i-n-j-u-r-e-d. No one else had died and police tested one driver for a-l-c-o-h-o-l.

The box started flashing again. 60 seconds remaining. 59. 58. He could pay for more time, but his mother would question why he had run out of spending money for the week by Wednesday, plus he didn't want to make the attendant suspicious, in case she might start paying attention to him and report him to the school. He grabbed his bag and walked past the front desk. The pink-haired girl was painting her fingernails a shiny purple while watching a soap opera on her computer.

Outside, Chen Long felt vulnerable in his school uniform. He equally felt bored, shuffling slowly down the sidewalk, nibbling his cold *baozi*. There were five more hours until the end of the school day and then he was supposed to go spend another hour and a half in English class before returning home. He no longer wanted to share the news about the phone call with Sarah.

"Chen Long! Hi!"

Shocked, he looked up to see Sarah standing right in front of him, a big grin on her face. "What are you doing here? Is today a holiday? Is that why you're not in school?"

She paused for him to answer, still smiling at him like she did when he got a perfect score on a quiz.

"Hello, Teacher Sarah. I...I am..."

"It's okay. I won't tattle on you for skipping school. I used to cut class a lot my freshman year."

"Yes," Chen Long muttered.

"Is something wrong? You don't look good. What is it?" Sarah tilted her head towards him, her light brown hair slipping over her shoulder.

Behind Sarah, Chen Long could see the Number 22 bus steadily making its way towards them. He wanted to go home. He didn't care if his mother knew what he had done that morning, and he didn't want to speak any more English today, not to the university man and especially not to Sarah.

"I stop English class. You are kind teacher, and pretty. Good bye," he blurted out and then ran as fast as he could to the corner and into the street, the traffic light turning green when he was halfway through the intersection, so that a fury of beeping horns shrieked in his ear as he hustled onto the curb. The bus had already stopped, and he frantically waved his arms at the driver as he sprinted the last few meters. Panting, he pulled the fare out of his pocket and then collapsed in a seat.

As the bus lurched back into traffic, he looked out of the window to see Sarah standing on the sidewalk. Her wide eyes met his as the bus passed and she waved, her lips moving with a message that he would never hear.

* * * *

At his apartment building, the daytime hallway was quiet, no sounds of cooking or cleaning or squabbling that were always present in the evenings. With a shaky hand, Chen Long unlocked his apartment door and cautiously peered inside.

"Chen Long?" his mother called out. "Why are you home so early?"

As he entered, he saw her sitting on their faded brown couch, her legs tucked under a pillow and a tissue in her hand. Stepping closer, he noticed her eyes were red and puffy. "Oh, my boy, come here," she called, stretching her arms out towards him.

Chen Long sunk down onto the couch next to his mother, and as he heard her start crying again, he tucked his head into the crook of her shoulder and sobbed as if he were three years old again and had just scraped his knees falling on the playground.

The next day, Chen Long informed his parents that he didn't want to take English classes anymore.

QUICKSILVER

ALLEN FRASER CLARK

Ah, that's the morning's rub:
A sky like mud, when what I want
is the smack of blue light hard enough
to marry air and water, turn this grey
as green as crayon. I want the day
to turn like a door on a slack hinge into

an afternoon with a front-row bullring seat.
Just an hour or two, *sombra y sol* in perfect
balance, not this stagnant stalled-out dark.
I want to bang a bright drum, be wild
and reckless, even risk samsaric breach.
I want to blow this dam, release
its flow to flood the earth.

LESS HERE

BRIAN THEDELL

Like the clotted sky as it strains in its weight,
and loses itself in bits, as rain—
Like the grain by grain march of sand off the bar
as each rolls to the ocean floor—

Like the warming wood core of the log and the flame,
the embers that smolder through years of rings—

So are all my moments with you.

Last week when you brushed against my shoulder,
I think I lost at least a year, and
Two days ago, just talking, your voice grabbed me
 just so
—I forgot what listening to anyone else was, and

Then just last night again, I think I told a random
 joke, you laughed,
and I forgot everything I thought I needed to say.

I am always forgetting myself these days.

The minutes between our meetings pass as moments
  then hours
then days, the distance between us shrinks and
  swells like the tides
at the call of the moon, and my thoughts turn back
  to you like a
rabbit to a secret hole just before the fangs catch.

I can't even imagine who I am anymore.

Let's breathe me away like desperate divers on their
  last tank,
let's set me alight like a midnight flare on the desert
  floor,
let's rev me, race me, plunge me down the freeway
  until
fumes and speed and steel are all that's left.

Hold me, please, until I'm
less here.

SCHIZOPHRENIA'S DAUGHTER: A NOVEL BASED ON A TRUE STORY

EXCERPT BY LESLIE FERGUSON

Chapter 8

My brother was climbing the birch tree in my grandparents' front yard, and I was in the upside-down part of a cartwheel, when my mom drove up to the curb. She didn't care that her car was on the wrong side of the street to be against the curb like that. The window on our side was rolled all the way down, and she leaned toward us.

"Kids," she said. "Get in the car. Hurry."

I could see that she had a white bandage wrapped around her wrist when she put her arm out to pull the lock up. Her other hand was on the steering wheel. The wrist of that arm was bandaged, too. It had only been a few days since the knife incident in the middle bedroom that nobody talked about, but I was pretty sure the bandages were because she'd cut her wrists.

I thought about the white lines across her wrists. She'd said they were scars she got from before I was born. This made me feel a little better because at least it wasn't my fault she wanted to die. Something else in the past made her feel like killing herself. Then why did I feel so responsible?

Philip jumped out of the tree and ran to the car.

"Don't," I said. "Stay back." I looked at my mom and stayed closer to the house. "You can't be here," I shouted. "Gramma said."

"Just get in the car, now." My mom said it like she was in a big hurry. But I knew it was because she was trying to take us and drive away before Gramma and Grampa could stop her.

"I'm getting Gramma," I said, and went to the screen door. I turned to open it, but my Gramma was already standing there, and Grampa had come right behind her. They both came out onto the grass.

My gramma put her arm out flicked her wrist like she was shooing a fly. "Go on, Rhoberta," she said. "Get out of here. We've had enough. Stop harassing us. You can't have them. You're not well."

And then my mom drove off, used the neighbor's driveway to turn around, and sped down the street.

"Come on, kids," Grampa said. "Get inside. We're done for the day." He went into the house first, and then my gramma, and then me and my brother.

The sky was blue and all the dirty, flowery smells of spring were in the air. It was still winter, but spring was coming, and it had been such a perfect day for playing outside.

* * * *

A few weeks passed. Philip and I were attending school regularly for the first time in over two years. It seemed like a "normal" family life for us meant living with our grandparents and without our mom.

We all began to relax, and we thought that maybe our mom really was going to leave us alone. After she tried to take us away, Gramma and Grampa used the word "harassment" every time they talked about maybe letting Mom come over to visit us. They said they just weren't up for it, and that more time "without incident" needed to pass before they could trust her.

And then, one day, at recess, while I was swinging high on a swing, I saw my mom standing outside the school's fence. Her fingers gripped the chain link tightly. I thought she might be trying to lift the fence out of the cement and throw it across the playground.

She wore an orange and pink paisley scarf to hold down her hair, and oversized sunglasses. She was the most stylish person in our family. And even when she was trying to steal me, she was beautiful.

"Leslie," she said. Her voice rushed out of her face in a strained, harsh, and deep sound, like maybe she didn't mean for it to come out that way but somehow it did anyway and once it was out, she couldn't do anything about it but let it be.

I was off the swings by now but standing on the safe side of the fence staring at her. The way her scarf blew a little in the breeze made me want to run to her.

"Leslie, come on. It's time to go." Her voice sounded normal this time. "Come around and get in the car. Hurry."

"No," I said. I shook my head to show that I meant it. "I'm getting my teacher." I turned away. And then I heard her voice again.

"Do what I say, Leslie. It's very important that you listen to me. We have to go."

I turned toward her again. I'm not sure why. And that's when I saw my brother sitting in the passenger's seat. He just looked at me.

"It's ok. Gramma and Grampa know I'm picking you up. They said it's okay."

I figured it *was* OK, if Gramma and Grampa knew about it and said it was okay, so I relaxed a little. I ran around to the skinny opening in the fence by the office and squeezed through.

Mom had Fritos and Pepsi for me when I got in the car. We drove and drove for what seemed like hours.

When it started to get dark, I said, "What are we doing? Where are we going?"

"Vegas," Mom said. "But first, Apple Valley. It's where Sherry lives. You remember my girlfriend Sherry, don't you? She used to live down the street from Auntie Philys."

It was twilight when we pulled into the driveway. At the front door, my mom bent down and pulled up the doormat to get a key out from under it.

The house was dark and cold. My mom switched on the kitchen lights. They buzzed a little.

"Be quiet inside," she said.

I looked out to the backyard and saw a large trampoline.

"Can we jump on it?" I asked.

My mom didn't answer, but she didn't stop us, either. Philip and I climbed on, alternating our jumps and then trying to get in sync. I jumped and laughed until my breathing was heavy and my legs ached and it was so dark I could barely see the edge of the trampoline. I wished we had a trampoline of our own, just like I'd always wished we had a pool of our own. There were so many things I wished.

We must have been at Sherry's for a couple of hours, but she hadn't come home.

"When are we going home?" I said. "Gramma and Grampa must be wondering where we are."

"I told you, they said it was okay," my mom said. "Now, stop talking about Gramma and Grampa. Aren't you glad you're with me and we're reunited as a family? Mommy's missed you so much." She was leaning against the kitchen counter, smoking a cigarette, and came closer to hug me and Philip at the same time.

"I'm hungry," I said.

"Me, too," said Philip.

My mom opened the kitchen cupboards one at a time until she found bread and peanut butter. She pulled a knife out of one the drawers, and a jar of strawberry jelly from the fridge.

"Peanut butter sandwiches, it is," she said. She untied the bag of bread and let her cigarette dangle from her lips.

The ash grew long like a snake firework on Fourth of July. We used to watch them squirm in the street before they died.

"Mom," I said, "your ashes are gonna fall into my sandwich."

"Here." She pushed the bread, jelly, and peanut butter towards me along the counter. "Make it yourself, then."

I made sandwiches for all three of us. Philip and I stood in the kitchen as we ate. My mom didn't eat hers. She stood watching us with squinty eyes through cigarette smoke.

We left the ingredients on the counter, and I put the knife in the sink.

"What now?" I said.

"Nothing," my mom said. "We wait."

"For what?" Philip said.

"For tomorrow, when it's safe to get back out on the road." My mom was staring at the television, but it wasn't even turned on. It was like she was looking at the glare and slices of light and movements we created. She closed the drapes, and we sat there in Sherry's living room, staring at each other and nothing, while the kitchen lights buzzed.

After I don't know how long, my mom finally said something. "Okay, time to go."

"But it's not morning," I said.

"Leslie," she yelled. "Can't you for once, just stop going against every. Single. Thing. And do what I say?"

It's just that nothing she said or did ever made any sense to me. And I didn't stop to think before speaking.

I thought back to the time she beat me up because she was trying to watch television, and I yelled to her from the bedroom because Philip kept kicking my bed up so it popped out of the top bunk frame. I thought my mattress was going to fall on him with me on top of it.

I kept screaming, "Mom! Mom!" And my bed finally fell, but only one end, and I slid at an angle, down to the bottom.

And she came in and grabbed me off my bed by my ponytail. That was when she beat me so hard I thought I would die.

I didn't want to get beat up this time, so I just shut up. I was already scared because there were knives in the house, and I didn't know if she might get the sharp ones like she did when she cut herself up in the middle bedroom at Gramma and Grampa's.

I just never knew what was going to happen. Mostly, she didn't hurt us, but the possibility of it hung over me always, like a rain cloud, heavy and ready to burst. I knew she was capable. And I knew she wasn't well. And that meant I could never predict her next move.

I stopped trying to fight.

She made us leave Sherry's and get back into the car. We started driving again.

"Are we going to Gramma's?" Philip said.

I was glad he said it because, it was what I wanted to

know but I didn't want to make Mom madder at me than she already was.

"We'll be there soon," Mom said. "We have to keep driving for now so they don't find us."

"Who?" he said.

"The government," Mom said. "We've been over this before. See all those bright headlights approaching? They never stop? Those are the semi-trucks. Big-rigs. That's the message from the government that they are on to us and we better keep running."

"They're just trucks, Mom," I said. I couldn't help it. I didn't care if she was mad. I was just annoyed. I had to make her understand. "That's what they *do, drive*. And it's dark now, so they have their headlights on. Duh." Why did she have to make everything so difficult?

"That's what they want us to believe," she said. "That's why it works. It has to be something that's easy to fool people with—the general public. We're smarter than that. They hide behind all these machines and medical procedures and political agendas. And the trucks are their way of telling us they're going to ram into us before they rape us and hang us by our feet. Philip knows, don't you, my sweet boy?" He was sitting in the passenger seat. She turned to face him. I could the whites of her teeth as she smiled.

"Uh-huh," Philip said in a slow, low voice. She patted his left leg with her right hand and then punched the lighter knob in the dash. A ring of orange glowed, and when it popped, she removed it and brought it to the cigarette she had just placed in her mouth. There was a singeing sound as she set the tip of her cigarette on fire. Fresh smoke filled the car, and my lungs burned.

We had been driving too long for me to reasonably think we would be going back to my Grandparents' house in Downey. My stomach growled and my eyelids were heavy. "I'm hungry. When are we going to eat?"

"You just had a sandwich," my mom said.

"I know," I said, "but that was forever ago."

We pulled into a Stater Bros. grocery store parking lot. We went to the back of the store to use the restroom. Then, in the aisles, I grabbed a bag of Oreos. Philip asked Mom to get a bag of Mother's Animal Circus from the top shelf. I wandered off on my own without realizing it and spotted a miniature baby doll in a sky blue polyester dress. She had a beanie body and plastic arms, legs, and head. I picked her up and held her. She fit in the palm of my hand. A helpless little baby.

"Put her back," Mom said.

I ignored her and carried the baby around with me while Mom grabbed some Pepsi and stared at some apples. At checkout, I laid my baby on the conveyor belt.

"I told you to put that back," Mom said. "*Kids*," she said to the cashier and shook her head.

"No," I said, and got ready to look her right in the eye. She laughed unevenly and handed the cashier some money. And I got my baby doll.

In the car, I ate some Oreos and caressed my hairless doll. I tried to look more closely at her face every time another car passed, letting flashes of light in. She looked so sweet, her face frozen in happiness. She was so small. I couldn't get over how small she was. And how perfect. And how mine...

The next thing I remember, my mom was calling my name.

"Leslie, wake up," she said

"Are we there?" I said. I felt dizzy.

"Not yet," she said. "Here, sit up." I realized the car was not moving. At some point while I was sleeping, she'd pulled off the road, and now we were parked somewhere in the pitch black dark in the middle of nowhere. "This is important. Listen very carefully, both of you."

I rubbed my eyes. I could barely feel my nose, and my hands were stiff and cold.

"What?" I said. I panicked. My baby! Where was she? I felt all over the seat and in the cracks. Then I put my hand as far under my mom's seat as I could reach.

I started to cry.

"Take this," she said.

"What is it?" I said as she dropped two little white pills into my hand.

"Nothing," she said. "It's just something to help you stay awake." She handed me a Pepsi.

"No," I shook my head. "I don't want to. I don't want to take any pills."

"Leslie," she said in her meanest, firmest voice. It was growly, like a bear had gotten in there, or a monster, and was trying to take over. "Do what I say. I am your mother. It is my job to protect you. It is very important that you listen to me and do what I say."

"No, p ease." I said. I was blubbering now. I didn't trust her. I thought if I took pills she gave me I might never wake up.

"Leslie!" Her shout made me jump.

"Did Philip take them? Philip, did you take them?" I said, trying to figure out if they were teaming up to kill me.

"Yeah," he said. "I took the same thing, and I'm fine, see?"

I believed him, and I trusted him, but I still was not going to take any pills. I pretended to put them in my mouth and took a gulp of Pepsi. I put my hand down and dropped the pills onto the floor of the back seat, hoping they would make it all the way under my brother's seat so my mom wouldn't find out I lied.

"Good girl," my mom said. "Now open your mouth and show me. And lift your tongue."

I showed her my empty mouth.

"Okay, good. Here's what's going to happen," my mom said. She sounded the most serious and clear she had all day. I looked at her eyes in the rearview mirror. "We are going to stay here in this parking lot."

I looked around. Where were we? Would anyone hear me if I screamed?

"And I'm going to get out of the car," she said. "And one of you is going to drive. I'm going to lie down on the ground and you're going to drive the car right over my head. Okay? Okay. Which one of you wants to do it?" She looked at my brother and then she turned around to look at me for real instead of in the mirror.

"What?" I said. "No. No way. Neither one of us are going to do it. That's crazy. What are you talking about? We don't even know how to drive."

"It's easy," she said. "I'll lie down right in front of the tire, and all you have to do is step on the gas. It'll be over real fast."

There was silence for a moment, and the windows were getting all fogged up. And I thought my heart was going to burst.

"I'll do it," Philip said.

"What? No," I said. My heart was beating super-fast, now, even faster than it did when I was jumping on the trampoline. "No, just stop it. Stop saying it. Stop agreeing with everything she says." I was crying now, wishing I knew where my baby doll was, wishing she could protect me, but she couldn't. She was just a stupid little doll with a stupid plastic face and a stupid beanie body in a stupid blue dress. She was no comfort to me now.

"You'll die," I said, through a bubble of snot in my throat. "Then what'll happen to us if you're dead?"

"It would just be easier that way," Mom said. "And then maybe they will go easier on you."

"Okay," Philip said once more. "If it's what you want.

Come on, Leslie. Just do what Mommy says."

"No," I said. I shook my head hard from side to side. It felt like something in there was rattling. It was all stuffy and achy. "Philip, stop it!" I screamed it so loud, the words scraped my throat. "Mom, nobody is going to drive over anybody's head."

"Okay," Mom said. It was that simple, as if I had only just told her there were no more Oreos left in the bag.

"I have another idea," Mom blurted. "I could just strangle you two, and that way you won't have to suffer any torture. And then I'll find a way to kill myself afterwards. Who wants to go first?"

"Mom, stop it. You're scaring me," I said. "You can't strangle me." *She would do it, too,* I thought. I remembered the time I woke up to her sitting next to me, and she had one of my red knee-high socks pulled tight around my neck. She was killing me in my sleep.

"I'll go," Philip said.

"That's my good boy," Mom said.

"Shut up," I yelled. "God, why do you always have to agree and go along with everything she says? Stop it. Nobody is going to get strangled. Everybody just shut up." The tears came again, and sickness filled my stomach. I thought I would throw up, or explode, or die from trying to make everybody stop saying crazy things.

"Well," my mom said. "If you won't cooperate, there's only one thing left to do."

"What's that?" my brother said.

"Keep running." And my mom started the car.

Where *was* my baby doll? I panicked. I knew she couldn't help me, really, but I still needed to know where she was. And I felt bad for thinking she was stupid. What had she ever done to me? She was just a sweet little innocent baby doll. I had to find her.

I checked the cracks of the seat again, to see if she got stuck. I put my hand down both sides between the doors and the seats again, to see if she slid there. I ran my hands over the floor mats. It was so dark. She was nowhere.

I blindly felt under my mom's seat again, to see if I had missed her the first time. Then I remembered I hadn't checked under Philip's seat.

I wiped her off on my pant leg, cradled her in my palm, held her up to my cheek, gave her a kiss.

She smelled like cigarette ashes and dirty car stuff, but I could have fit her whole head in my mouth if I really wanted to.

WHEN HE LEAVES

ALLIE GOVE

"The crease this water pail has worn in her palm,
what will that line mean to her life?"
                                            –Carolyn Forche

she does not follow him, but scales
a silver stitching on the hillside, thick ribbon
through the trees. He will come back
and she knows it. But there are empty jars
at the ends of streams. Afternoon pickets
into a slumber; night comes sliding
down the hill into her house
where she is dragging the furniture
into the dirt outside—she is not waiting.

SILENCE

ANTHONY JESSE

If fate had a voice, it would not be the elegant polyphonic lines of Bach or the crashing chords of Beethoven. It would be the space between the beats—the excruciating expectation of that next note. How many of us have spent more time pondering Nietzsche's tree than the ones that stand in our own front yards? And outer space is utterly silent, they say, there being no medium through which sound can travel. I imagine myself in that perpetual free-fall screaming in the dark at distant stars, unable to hear my own voice, unable to bear that gap in the conversation that forms light years between us.

DEUS EX MACHINA

DAVID J. SCHMIDT

God and Lucifer sat typing at their twin desks.

Lucifer paused and glanced over his laptop to catch God's eye. "Still no word from them, huh?"

God wiped the drops of espresso foam from His beard and looked up. "It's only been three weeks since we sent them the first draft. You know how these editors are."

"We worked on that piece for months. They haven't even sent us a courtesy notice. Maybe we should call them?"

God's eyes twinkled. "Be patient."

Lucifer added a third packet of Splenda to his coffee and stirred it anxiously.

* * * *

"It's here, it's here!" Lucifer was clutching the manila envelope, scattering bills across the floor as he ran toward the office. God set His cup down on the saucer with a light "clink" and took the package from Lucifer. The return address bore the publisher's standard label, written in

Hebrew: "Prophetic Books, Ltd."

God pulled the manuscript out of the envelope and set it on the table; He held the editor's cover letter up to the light of the lamp.

Messrs. God and Lucifer,

We are pleased to present you with the final draft of your manuscript, tentatively titled "Job Shrugged." You may find that some minor editorial changes have been made; this is for purely professional and technical reasons...

God read further down the text of the cover letter as Lucifer rifled through the returned manuscript. Silence hung in the air. Lucifer stared at the last page of the packet in disbelief. "You've got to be kidding me."

God leaned in over his shoulder. "I was afraid of this," He muttered, unsurprised.

"Don't they even know the meaning of the phrase 'artistic integrity'?! How can they just change it like this?"

"You'd be surprised how often it happens." God adjusted the spectacles on His nose.

"But...Look at this stupid tag they added at the end of the story! They didn't even bother to make the tone match the rest of the book. It just pops up out of nowhere. They must think our readers are a bunch of morons!"

"It's their call, Lucifer. They're the publishers."

"You have to do something about this, God. We'll sue them for all they're worth."

God calmly took another sip from the demitasse on his oak desk. "We're not going to do that."

Lucifer reached for the editorial cover letter; God held it at arm's length. "I don't think you want to read the rest of this, Lucifer, with the mood you're in. It'll just depress you."

* * * *

God and Lucifer sat by the fireplace later that evening. God was enjoying a Macanudo cigar with a glass of Scotch. A violin and guitar duo played on the stereo.

"I'm telling you," God said, "this is how the business is. They do this sort of thing all the time. It doesn't matter how artificial it sounds, how ad hoc...they always feel the need to add on a happy ending that explains everything. They want to wrap it up into a nice, neat package."

"But..." Lucifer took another sip from his can of Four Loko. "That goes against everything in the literary handbook! We had such a finely crafted story. We explored human suffering without offering any easy answers. All the tragedy Job suffers, his friends trying to comfort him with religious platitudes, his encounter with the Divine...and then the editors go and ruin it with this fairy-tale ending. Job suddenly gets back everything he lost..."

"I understand exactly how you feel. Trust Me. It's almost a rule of this industry. Take a look over here..."

God slid His cigar to the edge of the ashtray and drew a crude graph in the ash, using the tip of His pencil to trace two intersecting vectors. "This line here is the honesty of the writing. Now this one going downwards...this is the number of people that are willing to stomach the writing."

Lucifer's skinny jeans tightened against his thighs as he leaned in closer. "Inversely proportional."

"I'd be lying to you if I said it gets easier with time," God sighed. "Especially when you've really labored over a story."

Lucifer's eyes suddenly lit up. "Wait, I've got it—we'll just cut the editors out of the equation entirely! Fuck 'em. If they can't handle a story that doesn't have a sticky sweet Pollyanna conclusion, we'll self-publish it."

"Sorry. That's not how it works."

Lucifer threw his hands up and his vaporizer issued a puff of smoke into the air. "Are You high? If You're worried about that contract you signed with them, I know plenty of lawyers..."

"I stand by My contract, you know that."

"You're impossible."

God stood up and faced the fire. "Look at it this way," He began softly. "They need an explanation. They can't handle mystery and ambiguity."

"You're not helping," Lucifer fumed.

God leaned against the mantle and turned slowly. "What I'm getting at is this—what if they had the maturity to deal with ambiguity? If they didn't need to always feel like things had an explanation, if they didn't need to blame someone for all their incomprehensible misfortune...well you'd be out of a job pretty quick, now wouldn't you?"

Lucifer stared into the fire for a minute. His eyes slowly acquired their old glow. When he stood to put his jacket on, he had a new spring in his step. "I get it," he said with a smile.

"You off to work?" God asked.

"You bet." Lucifer jingled his car keys and walked toward the door. "We still on for Taco Tuesday tomorrow?"

"I wouldn't think of missing it," God chuckled.

And Lucifer headed off into the darkness to spread sickness and hunger and poverty. This evening, more than most evenings, he was looking forward to his night job. He knew that this was one area where he was sure to receive full credit for his work.

RULES FOR EATING PISTACHIOS

BARBARA HUNTINGTON

Pistachios
Fresh from the co-op
In a pottery bowl shaped by an artistic friend
He's now a dentist
His art—crowns and dentures

Don't crack shells with your teeth!

Gorging
I make a rule for myself:
I may savor the salty insides
'til empty shells fill my palm
If a shell falls
I cease my feast

I pry open another nut
A single shell falls to the floor
But if I were careful
My palm could cradle more

Rule revision:

I retrieve the shell back to my palm
Pick apart another pistachio
And another
I will my hand to hold one more,
Coax open a reluctant nut

Shells splatter to the floor
My palm is empty
The bowl of pistachios isn't

Rules be damned!

JUST LIKE HOME

MARY J. FRY

I swam here from another place. After the crash of 2009, I drove though the sinuous arteries of Los Angeles to San Diego, landing here like a wild-eyed fish, rolling over to see palm fronds that looked like they were on fire in the late afternoon sun. Then weeping like sympathetic spindly purple friends in the evening. It was not home, but a place to wait for death. Not mine, but my brother's. I would just breathe in my bed at night. It seemed I could never sleep. I could not help him. He was bound for destruction. Like a bullet in the chamber. He would go like so many great writers, but this bullet and the wrapped manuscript was not ready, but the bullet sometimes blows too soon.

In the hospital again, my father went to get him and drove him to the V.A. hospital for rehab. He didn't know why my father brought him there. Knowing he could not hold him there at home, my father took him to the airport, watching him turn and give a weak wave as he boarded the plane. My father thought he would never see him alive. He was going to hit bottom—and die there.

It was always late at night when my brother would call. Sometimes I did not pick up the phone. He was writing, he was drinking, and that was all. The words, so dear to him, were his solace and the devil himself.

Then the call came. He was in the hospital again, and I went to see him. He would pull a Macgyver, a miraculous breakout of the tubes and devices keeping him humming. But instead he kept talking about pulling the plug in his sardonic way. As I looked at his yellow-skinned face he told me he accepted what was to come, that his soul was black. But maybe he knew that there was only way to be clean again. We all collect so much dust along the way, some more than others.

Then his eyes looped around the room, following pleasing hallucinations. The morphine had kicked in. He was beyond me.

I came back to San Diego and lay there in bed, still breathing. It was incomprehensible. I had no brother. How could that be? And I was alone. But I didn't want to go to a grief group—I didn't want to be around sad people. I didn't want to be around me. Then a kind of miracle happened. I met someone, a young man, very young, way too young. He did not understand my grief, and I knew he would not stay. He would arrive at my door, all dudish, torn jeans, tousled curly hair. We walked along Mission Beach at night, salt-water bubbles popping at our feet. It was chilly, and I held to him. Christmas was approaching. Looking at the lights strung up on balconies lining the shore, he informed me that it was all code for magical mushrooms." Yule tree— what grows under trees?—mushrooms! Santa flying in the air—mushrooms!" Of course! I had no idea my family and I were celebrating illicit hallucinogenic organic material all these years. I had to tell my mother right away. She might want to rethink the menu.

Then came the inevitable. The young man told me his chakras had gone awry, it was no good, and he was breaking up with me. He had bought an old van. His dream was to live in this old VW Beetle down at the beach. Be the dude. Be the Lebowski. Drop out.

But he had made me feel better, like floating over the worst part. I inherited my brother's writing. I wrote the screenplay that we started together before he was too far gone, along with the manuscript he left me. He would like that.

Strangely, I'll be talking about my brother and all of his e-mails will suddenly show up on my computer screen or an old Facebook post with his picture will suddenly display in my feed. Unfettered by the crust of life, I imagine him seeping into hardware circuitry and playing with the 1s and 0s, just to say hello. All is well. He's back to his old Macgyver tricks, just like home.

IN A LONELY PLACE

CHERYL HEINEMAN

–For Dix Steele

It's easy to look back.
The rear view mirror tells it was slant love,
that he was dynamite waiting to explode.

I noticed him at the piano bar.
Nice suit, bow tie, brandy, cigarette.
I liked his face, the color of his eyes,
the shape of his head.

He saw the ring on my left
hand, my man on my right,
but as he passed by he whispered
"You shouldn't have done it honey,
no matter how much money
that pig's got." He slipped his
number into my velvet purse.

I shadowed him home
to his apartment at the dark end
of a tightly-curved road.

He was artsy, steps above
my husband, a popcorn salesman.

He was a writer.
Suspicion, murder, cadavers on fur rugs,
dead girls in dangling pearl earrings
lying like long lonely staircases.

His steel hands took my face.
He said he'd been looking
for me for a long time.

This morning, I left satin headboards,
iron gated rooms with slatted loneliness
and headed home to my grapefruit-blond world.

Yesterday, I'd have married a guy like that.
Today, I don't have the imagination.
A lonely courtyard separates us.

But last night, for a few hours, I lived.

LÁVESE LAS MANOS

CLAIRE HSU ACCOMANDO

Lávese las manos, the sign says
in the ladies' room, in ink, above
the sink. Wash the hands, is scribbled
on the mirror with purple lipstick.

Yes, wash *las manos* that fill and fold
enchiladas and burritos. If need be, wear
nitril gloves. Sanitize, rubberize, vinylize.
Sheath in latex the hands delivering newborns.

Keep warm the little biscuit fist
that some day may pitch a baseball
flying at an insane speed.
Perfume the palms that caress.

Insure the robust paws of the boxer.
Also the agile digits of the pianist.
Steady the fingers that hold the scalpel,
or the cutting tool of the bomb diffuser.

Stop the index poised on the trigger. Scrub
splattered blood from the underside of fingernails.

Disinfect the hands that clamp electric probes
to the genitals of enemy combatants,

while a new order Pontius Pilate
asks for a basin of scented water
and a fluffy designer towel.
Lávese las manos, the sign says.

Excerpt from

THE STAINED-GLASS WOMAN, V.1

*a multigenerational family saga about former
Amish, medical malpractice, sociopaths,
and identical twins reared apart*

DIANA AVERY AMSDEN

* * * *

Chapter 36. DARRYL YODER

*"To lose one parent may be regarded as a misfortune;
to lose both looks like carelessness."*
Oscar Wilde

Early Monday afternoon, September 30, 1940, Nadia Esmand's cousin, eight-year-old Darryl Yoder, was staying with his maternal grandparents, the Pollifaxes, in Glendale while his parents, Bob and Antoinette, enjoyed a much-needed vacation. Papa was an attorney, planned to run for judge, and wanted to be well rested.

Darryl was in the third grade in a private school, and his grandparents had kept him home today because his parents were returning. They would fly into the Atlantic and Telegraph Airport, get their car, pick up Darryl, and head home.

Mama and Papa had told Darryl they were considering getting him a baby sister or brother. Darryl had said, "Let's get twins like Aunt Mariam did, a boy and a girl!"

Mama had said, "It's possible, but I think we'll get only one or the other."

Papa had told Darryl, "You'll be a big brother. Your little brother or sister will look up to you and try to be like you, so you must be a leader and teacher and set a good example. You must be a protector too, protect your little brother or sister from meanies who like to tease kids, or hurt them, or pick on them, or take their things."

Darryl's chest had swelled. He had felt brave and proud and wise and strong.

At lunch, Darryl told his grandparents, "I wish Mama and Papa were bringing me back a baby brother or sister today, but I know you get babies at hospitals. They went on a hunting trip. When they go hunting, they bring back something to eat. Last time they brought back ducks and Mama made duck à l'orange. It was so good!"

"I prefer pheasant or grouse or dove," said Grandma.

"I'd take a venison steak or boar roast, but with what it costs Bob and Antoinette to hunt," grumbled Grandpa, "the meat they bring back costs as much as caviar."

After lunch, Darryl and his grandparents went into the living room, where Darryl sat down on the big hooked rug and dumped his Tinkertoys out of their cylindrical box. "I'm going to make an airplane like Papa's. He took me up once, and held me in his lap and let me handle the controls and fly for a minute. It was exciting. I felt like Superman. Papa says when I'm eighteen, he'll teach *me* to fly.

"Papa says a good pilot is a good mechanic, and carefully checks out his plane himself before every flight. He showed me the engine and told me the names of the parts and what each one does. He handed me his checklist, and had me read each step out loud to him. He showed me how he checked each thing, always in the same order."

His bald, skinny grandfather harrumphed and switched on the "cathedral" radio, shaped like a Gothic arch. Tchaikovsky's *Symphonie Pathétique* was playing.

Grandma sat down on the maroon velveteen couch against the mustard-yellow and algae-green velveteen cushions and set her sewing basket on the coffee table. She pulled one of Darryl's blue socks over a wooden knob she called an "egg," and started darning. "You keep wearing holes in your heels," she complained. Her silver eyeglass rims matched her hair, which she still wore in a bob, although bobs were no longer fashionable. "When your *mother* was your age, she *never* wore holes in *her* socks. She read or played the piano. You should stay inside more."

"Stay inside, keep your clothes clean, do your homework and read," said Grandpa, who sat in *his* chair, a matching wingback, filled his pipe, and started puffing. He peered over his rimless glasses. "So you want to fly an airplane, like your father. You even look like a pint-size copy of him. Wish you were more like Antoinette."

Darryl loved being outside. He enjoyed slides, swings,

monkey bars, tag, hide-and-seek, blind-man's bluff, running races, playing ball with other kids, and exploring. Sometimes he hurt himself, but never badly. He gently fingered the big scab on his right knee where he had scraped it yesterday playing in the backyard at home. It was the same color as the living room upholstered furniture, the color of dried blood.

The somber radio music made him sad. He could hardly wait for his parents to come and take him away from these gloomy boring people who always made him sit still and never let him play outside. He thought his grandparents' bodies were disgusting. He was fascinated and repelled by the huge pores on their noses, hairs growing out of their nostrils and ears, calluses, and skin discolorations, so different from the smooth symmetrical little face he saw in the mirror, and the small, soft limbs he saw when he looked down.

Sometimes he looked up into Grandma's face and imagined the nostrils were eyes above the lips that moved when Grandma spoke.

"We interrupt this program for a local news flash."

Darryl's grandparents looked up. His grandmother laid down her darning egg. His grandfather took his pipe out of his mouth.

"At one-thirty this afternoon, a red sports airplane crashed into a house and fell burning in a yard in Los Angeles. Witnesses said the motor had been missing audibly and the plane was flying low in the light fog, apparently searching for the airport.

"Suddenly it dipped and clipped into the chimney of a

house. No one in the house was injured, but the plane crashed into the front yard and burst into flames. It was demolished before nearby fire departments could extinguish the blaze.

"The body of the pilot, identified as Robert Yoder, thirty-nine, was catapulted, a flaming comet, for 120 feet to thud against a house."

Darryl heard Grandma gasp, and Grandpa say, "Oh my God."

"Mrs. Yoder's body was found shrouded in a half-opened parachute. Apparently she had attempted to bail out, but the plane was flying too low for the parachute to carry her to safety. Witnesses said the plane carried no lights."

Darryl heard Grandma wail, "Antoinette!"

"Several rifle shells carried on the plane exploded when the craft became enveloped in flame. The couple had been on a hunting trip in northern California."

Darry watched Grandma rise from the couch and walk unsteadily toward Grandpa, accidentally kicking over and breaking Darryl's tinker toy airplane.

Grandpa rose and wrapped Grandma in his arms. Her anguished cries rang in Darryl's ears. Grandpa cradled her head, and murmured something in her ear.

Suddenly remembering Darryl, Grandma turned her head toward the bewildered, frightened boy looking up at them. He would never forget her agonized expression. Grandma said, "Don't worry, Darryl. Grandpa and I'll take care of you."

To Darryl, Grandma's voice had the sound of doom.

* * * *

After the funeral and interment, Grandpa Pollifax drove Grandma back to their home. Before Grandpa got out of the car, he said to his wife, "Bob must have skipped checking his engine, or didn't do a very good job. He killed our Antoinette."

Darryl, in the back seat, said, "It wasn't Papa's fault. It was an accident."

Before they could enter the house, a Western Union boy brought them a telegram.

The Pollifaxes stood in the foyer together to read it, Darryl looking up at them. A telegram meant something serious.

Grandpa said, "Genevieve and Fred Esmand want to adopt Darryl."

Darryl remembered Mama showing him snapshots of Aunt Genevieve, Uncle Fred, and his cousins in the family album. He remembered his uncle and aunt, who had left California four years earlier, when he was four years old. Uncle Fred made him a kite and a swing. His cousin, Nadia, had been only two, but she was a sweet little girl and it was fun to push her around in a doll carriage. She would now be six.

A year ago, Darryl's parents told him that Uncle Fred and Aunt Genevieve had a baby boy. Darryl's new cousin's name was Larry. *If Uncle Fred and Aunt Genevieve adopt me, I'll have both a little sister and a baby brother! I'll be a good boy. I'll be helpful and I'll protect Nadia and Larry from meanies.* The grief-stricken boy began to feel a glimmer of hope.

"Those selfish Esmands have two children," said Grandma. "We lost our only child, and they want to take her little boy away from us."

Grandpa said, "Genevieve doesn't even like children. She wants control of Darryl's inheritance. Bob's life insurance. Insurance on his airplane. Bob's and Antoinette's house. Their car. Their bank accounts and investments."

Grandma patted Darryl's hand. "Don't worry, dear. We won't give you up."

Darryl's last hope died.

He never recovered from the shock and loss.

Soon the Pollifaxes' monthly letters to Genevieve said that Darryl had begun to wet his bed, and he set fires.

Before a decade had passed, the letters said that Darryl had been kicked out of prep school because of his alcohol binges.

LETTER TO GEORGIA O'KEEFFE, 2015

CLAUDIA POQUOC

Dear Georgia,

You may not remember, (I could never forget),
we met at Lake George in the spring of 1919.
You were staying at the Stieglitz ranch painting
birch and red canna. I was there to write.
We'd meet at the beach or under the old oak,
wanting to keep our commingling a secret—
both of us longing for a private life.
You'd tell me how you were finally tired of finding,
yet, another shade of green to paint.
And I'd tell you I couldn't find a single word
to express your bottomless colors,
your amorous forms
or how you turned flowers into living bodies.
I hear you still have those two paintings of us—
bare butt cheeks rising like two moons over the lake.
What did you call them...*10* and *10A?*
Whatever happened to the last painting you did
before you left...

Together we named it, *Tree with Cut Limb.*
And too long now I've wondered when to reveal
the one poem I'd kept:

green hills rising
blood-red bulbs bursting
female cross-pollination

Forever yours,
Claudia

TOO LAZY TO BE SATAN

SUZANA NORBERG

The Cliff

The Ace bandage on my ankle must be choking off an artery. There's so much pulsing and throbbing going on inside my Victorian ankle boot that I wonder if any of the guests can see it. My right arm is slipped under my brother Tommy's left, and I'm leaning hard on him as we walk down the path to the clearing on the cliff. The dirt crunches under my boots like the soundtrack to a showdown at the OK Corral. The wind is trying to take my hat so I press it to my head with my free hand and hold. Between the wind and the limp, I feel off balance.

I spot my grandmother in the crowd. She's wearing a cobalt blue dress and a sour face. Her favorite expression is pffft and after a lifetime of pffft-ing, her face just kind of stuck there. She's the reason I didn't wear white. The reason I'm cream-colored from my veiled hat to my Victorian boots. I knew that if I wore white, Grandmother would probably announce to the wedding guests, in broken English, that I really shouldn't have.

That I am, after all, a *kurva*. It's Serbian for whore, and her favorite word to hock out of her throat.

Standing next to Grandmother in the crowd on the cliff is my mother, wearing a lavender dress and a pinched mouth. After a lifetime of muttering "Yes Master" to Grandmother's endless criticisms and commands, her face just kind of stuck there.

And then I see him. The slim, six-foot groom is heading toward me, to the center of the clearing on a cliff in Torrey Pines State Reserve in La Jolla, California. He's wearing a navy suit. In the four months we've dated, I've never seen him in a suit. And his comb-over is curiously wind-resistant. His hair was the first thing I noticed that day at the Chinese buffet when I met him. It was the oddest mop I'd ever seen—a Prince Valiant bob on the sides with a cotton-candy comb-over top. And he was wearing sunglasses in a dimly lit restaurant. I should have run right then, but I was taught to ignore my instincts, so I did. Eventually I began seeing the man and not the hair. But I'm seeing it now, on my wedding day.

Backlit by the sun, the groom's comb-over is a dark tangled halo and for the first time I see this man is old. I am young. I barely know him, and I don't particularly like his thin-lipped kisses or the way his nails are filed to guitar-pick points. Why can't he just use a guitar pick?

But he's born-again, so he must be good. He's witty, soft-spoken, and non-grabby—the only non-grabby man I ever met. He was such a gentleman that he wanted to wait until we were married to have sex. I'd never met a man like that before. After my dorm-room salvation, I tried not to be a fornicator, but it was hard. If you're married, you can't be a fornicator.

But still. I don't know him well. A month ago I was so nervous and uncertain, I told him I just wasn't sure I wanted to get married. He took it so well that it made me feel bad. "Don't worry about it," he'd said with a quiet dignity. Oh God. I would be dashing his hopes just like all the others. The ex-fiancé; the ex-business partner; his father. I felt terrible. I retracted.

But I don't owe him anything. I barely know him.

I want to run but can hardly walk and just need a minute to think because everything happened so fast. All these people came, and now I'm in too deep. The wind is trying to take my hat, so I'm holding on for dear life. Dear God please somebody step up and say you can't forever hold your peace.

I'd been asking God all along, Should I do this? Should I marry him? God didn't say. So when I fell in the alley just days before the wedding, falling for no reason at all, not tripping, not stumbling, yet twisting my left ankle so hard that I could barely drag myself back to civilization, I didn't take it as a message from God. Surely the creator of the universe would have better communication skills than smiting an ankle in an alley.

The wind is trying to take my hat, so I'm holding on for dear life. Dear God, please somebody step up and say you can't forever—What? Pastor Goode repeats a question.

God, please save me.

Waiting.

Waiting.

Nothing.

And so I say, "I do."

The wind carries my words, and the words carry my life over the cliff.

Ray of Sunshine

My primary career choice was actress, but I knew that would never fly with the family, so I majored in advertising. As a fan of the TV-show Bewitched, I thought I'd enjoy a Darren Stevens-like career, coming up with catchy phrases to help sell products. Even that was a stretch for Mother and Grandmother. As immigrants from Yugoslavia, they understood only clear-cut careers for women. Teacher. Nurse. *Prostitutka*. Plus everybody always knew somebody who couldn't get a job in advertising.

"It's very competitive," pointed out Mother in her Slavic accent. "Corrine's niece hez been trying for six years and kent find anything. Now she works in a nursing home. Changing bedpans."

Corrine's niece must have a severe lack of skills, I thought, or a loose definition of trying.

"If you kent find a job, maybe you could take a few klesses in nursing," offered Mother on the eve of my graduation. I was not aware that a medical career could be pursued casually. I pictured myself strolling down the halls of Milwaukee's Trinity Memorial Hospital, my name badge proclaiming Suzana Ignjatovic, Nurse Hobbyist.

Two days before graduation, I was hired by Greed & Associates (name changed to shield the greedy). I started work the day after graduation. The agency owner's son,

Greed Jr., thought I had potential as a copywriter, but said I had to start as a paste-up artist. No problem. I was thrilled to be spared a life of changing bedpans.

I wielded my T-square, X-acto blade, and rubber-cement brush with gusto. I went on donut runs, Xeroxed things, and obliged in all manner of gophering. I even secretly wrote and illustrated a dozen different ideas for the agency's high-profile Wisconsin State Fair account known for its punny billboards every summer. I couldn't wait to present my ideas when the time came. The Greeds loved them and used them. Gems like "Piggy's Back" and "Our Coop Runneth Over." By today's standards, nauseating; back then, award-winning. A year later I was still downstairs in the art department, pasting up ads.

When they discovered I could do funny voices from years of secretly mimicking parishioners of St. Nikola Serbian Orthodox Church with my brother Tommy, they started using me in radio commercials. From the Queen of England to hyperactive dingdongs or stern librarians, I summoned voices I didn't even know I had. This saved the Greeds from hiring a $50-per-hour voice talent, but I still didn't see a nickel more.

There was a constant push for new business, but once an account was acquired it lost all novelty and was shoved aside while we worked on new spec campaigns for new prospective clients. You had to account for every minute on your timesheet and you didn't dare have downtime, so you had to overstate how long everything took. How else could you cover for those extra 10 minutes to clean up the rubber-cement spill on aisle four? Or the 20 minutes to tourniquet your thumb when the tip got ripped off in a freak accident with a spring-loaded desk lamp?

My trip to see my brother Tommy in San Diego was just around the corner, and I couldn't wait to get out of Greedville for a week. My plan was to go on job interviews so that maybe I could give notice when I returned. I made a resumé that looked like a magazine ad featuring my snowmobile boots, with the headline: Mine feet have trod the glory of the wet Wisconsin snow; I've learned to jump-start batteries but now it's time to go.

Using a national directory from the library, I sent my resumé to every ad agency in San Diego. One was on a street called Camino de la Siesta. Applying shoddy bilingual skills acquired in fifth grade via Señorita Kowalski on KPBS-TV, I determined this was the Street of the Nap. It sounded delightful, like maybe margaritas were involved.

Two weeks before my trip, Greed Jr. called me into his office. I knew right away something bad would happen. Not only because he couldn't make eye contact but because he'd never summoned me to his office before. The more he pre-ambled, the louder the ringing in my ears and the less I could follow what he was saying. "...hired you...not working out...this is difficult..."

Slowly his message became clear. I—who got A's in every subject except phys ed due to spectacular uncoordination, who tied for second place as Most Likely to Succeed in Pulaski High's class of '79—WAS BEING FIRED FROM MY FIRST REAL JOB. I wanted so much to leave unaffected and with dignity but, as ever, my tear ducts sabotaged me.

By the time I got back to the art department I was crying

so hard I could barely blubber to my cube mates, "They fired me." Just then Ray came Clydesdale-ing down the stairs. Ray was the creative director, and wildly unstable, so we called him Ray-hole.

"He's bad meat in this town," Paddy liked to say.

Ray was fond of pounding down our stairwell so hard and fast that it sounded like he was falling, yelling things like "WHERE THE FUCK IS THAT AD?" Or "WHY IS THE LEADING SO FUCKING GAPPY? YOU COULD DRIVE A FUCKING TRUCK THROUGH IT."

Twenty minutes later he'd expect you to laugh at his imitation of Eddie Murphy as Buckwheat, or Joe Piscopo as Doug Whiner from Saturday Night Live, when in fact you were still trembling with fear and on the verge of bladder collapse. Or at least I was.

Every time I heard his voice, my Pavlovian armpits went damp.

Ray-hole came to express his condolences, peppered with suspect phrases such as, "I hope you don't blame me" and, "I didn't have anything to do with it." It didn't even occur to me, until then. "Come see me on your way out, buddy. Come to my office," said Ray-hole.

Buddy? Asshole.

I didn't go to his office. I didn't say goodbye. I drove home crying, took in the mail crying, sat in my studio apartment crying. (I moved away from home as soon as I got a job. Naturally I was accused of being a *kurva*. Why else would a young lady not want to live at home and sit on the scratchy polyester sofa translating All-Star Wrestling and

Little House on the Prairie to Grandmother?)

Then I noticed the canary-yellow corner of an envelope in the mail pile, with a return address on Camino de la Siesta. I stopped crying. I tore open the envelope and unfolded the matching yellow stationary of The Phillips Organisation, the agency on the street of naps and margaritas. The message was brief: Dear Ms. Ignjatovic, Call me when you get to town so we can arrange an interview. Sincerely, Bob Browand, Creative Director.

What were the odds of getting this letter on this day? It had to be a message from God. I was a believer in messages from God. My despair turned to euphoria, and I pressed my palms to my ears to tamp down the shiver that ran through me. A shiver of joy and disbelief at how life could change in an instant.

San Diego Furlough

My mother's main concern about my trip was the sleeping arrangement. In her mind, there was a fine and horrifying line between sleep and s-e-x. We never said words like that in our house. It was best to ignore such gruesome subjects in the hope they would go away.

When I was younger, before I even needed a bra and often forgot to wear an undershirt, Mother would lean forward and whisper in horror, "Suzi! Your brown spots are showing." I don't think I even learned the word nipple until eighth-grade biology class. Thank God there wasn't a molester in our family orbit. I would have been a prime target. Not only could I never have told anyone what happened, I didn't even know what my parts were called.

My brother Tommy had a roommate, so Mother thought it would be fah-nny if I slept on the couch. It was her Slavic-accented code word for anything even remotely sexual. "What if he comes home late and there you are? Wouldn't you feel...[big pause]...fah-nny?"

Via mere horizontalness, she saw the dreaded potential for lasciviousness. She suggested instead of on the couch, I should sleep with my brother. Now that would be fah-nny.

At six-foot-five, Tommy was hard to miss in the crowd at the arrival gate at Lindbergh Field, as was the giant hand that waved at me. When it was spread open like that you could almost see a basketball in it, but Tommy hated basketball. He reached his vertical destiny by age 16 and ever since, people have been asking, "You play basketball?"

Teachers. Classmates. Strangers. Old Serbian men at church; except they pronounced it besketboll. Tommy felt it was like asking short people if they were jockeys or miniature golfers.

With khaki shorts, flip-flops, a tank top, and sunglasses on a cord around his neck, Tommy looked nothing like the Milwaukee boy who left home a year earlier. He also had a dark tan. With brown eyes and coarse, curly brown hair, was my polar opposite in hue.

I had blue eyes, wavy dishwater-blond hair, and a touch of albino. I couldn't hold a tan, so I stopped even trying. I also probably looked like an American on a senior tour group in Paris, with my short-sleeved T-shirt, pleated-waist jeans, and white tennis shoes.

"Hhai Suuzi," said Tommy. His real name was Tomislav.

"Hhai Tomo." I called him Tomo. We always greeted each other in faux Serbian accents. It was just our way. We always kept it light, even during the darkest times at home. Even after a pants-peeing episode, courtesy of twin backhands from Bruno. His real name was Branislav but our father's American nickname perfectly captured his demeanor.

Bruno looked like a meld of Paul Newman and Steve McQueen, so he had that going for him. But he also operated off his brainstem, like a parakeet. With only a hint of stimulus, his medulla oblongata would sound the rage alarm. Even when he wasn't raging, Bruno was simmering— flicking his cigarette, fidgeting with his Zippo, rotating his thumbs, and licking the corners of his mouth. When he had a cigarette jammed in there, he'd walk it from left to right and back again, using his lips and teeth. The speed at which the cigarette walked—its glowing ember glaring at us all the way—was our indicator of his fury level.

He also blinked at a rate faster than the rest of us. Just before an outburst he'd blink even faster as the blue in his eyes frosted over.

Tommy and I were so terrified of Bruno that we'd pee in our pants at the mere bark of our names. It was an odd sensation. You'd try to tighten the muscle that seals your bladder from your urethra, but it's passed out on your pelvic floor. So you christen your shoes with warm fear.

Tomo flung his sunglasses over his shoulder and we hugged, my forehead level with his sternum. The only other times I hugged him were when he moved to San Diego, and when he went off to West Point Military Academy after high school. With straight A's, Tommy had no trouble securing the necessary endorsements from teachers, clergy and our congressman. He returned three weeks later and 20 pounds lighter. Even going in, Tommy knew he wasn't military material. He just wanted the free education, then decided it wasn't worth it.

"They shove it up your ass a nickel at a time," he said.

The drive down I-8 to Tommy's place was magical, lined with palm trees, sunshine, and salt air. I felt like the film had switched from black-and-white to Technicolor Oz. The salt air followed us into Tommy's apartment where the stereo was tuned to a Mexican radio station. Between American rock songs, the DJ said things like, "EF-eh EM-eh, TeeHWANA, Baja, ForCaliforRRneeah, MEHeekoh." There was also a lot of "poonto poonto eee nueveh."

I didn't know what it meant, but I loved it. It was nothing like the Sunday morning Serbian Radio Hour where every song was the same: hectic accordions, and singers with frantic Middle-Eastern warbles, probably picked up during the Turks' 500-year reign over the Serbs. Every Sunday, Grandmother hauled the big Sears Silvertone AM/FM radio to the kitchen table, just a foot away from where I was trying to eat my Kaiser roll with butter and apricot jam.

Between songs, orange-haired Olga Kostić would reel off the names of parishioners and the dollar amounts they'd contributed to the church. There were lots of names and dollar amounts. Olga's real voice was impossibly shrill, but somehow she managed to shrill it up a notch on the radio. Adding to the frenzy were constant massive static and occasional Outer Limits woo-woo sounds when Grandma tried to fine-tune the dial. By the time Sunday breakfast was over, my nerves were in tatters.

Tommy set me up with a map and a rental car, and for the next few days I went on interviews at local ad agencies. No one else sent a letter in response to my resumé, but most of the creative directors were willing to see me. I showed them the small but creative collection of ads I'd written, and two of the CDs said they'd use me as a freelancer if I lived in town. I was euphoric. San Diego was magic.

The sun shined every day. Freeways wound past palm trees and canyons, not factories and tanneries. Houses were white or pink stucco with red-tile roofs, not beige or gray clapboard with asphalt shingles. All around were succulents, rust-free cars, and waterfalls of magenta bougainvillea. I'd never even heard of bougainvillea before I came to visit Tommy.

It turned out there was nothing fah-nny about sleeping on the couch. Tommy's roommate was a completely normal guy. I even hemmed a pair of pants for him, as only the offspring of immigrants would.

Three days into my trip, Tommy invited me to join him and a few co-workers for lunch. So I did.

I pulled open the scuffed red door of the Super China Buffet and was temporarily movie-theater blinded. For the middle of the day, the place was surprisingly dark inside.

It took me a moment to spot Tommy. I just scanned the room for the tallest object and there he was. Even seated, Tommy was always the tallest.

"This is my sister," he said, introducing me to his three co-workers from the payroll department of General Dynamics. We were all in our early twenties except for one guy. The one I would come to know as Elmer Gantry, in homage to the immoral evangelist in the classic, eponymously named novel by Sinclair Lewis.

The Elmer Gantry of the Chinese buffet appeared to be 40 and had terrible hair. Longish sides with a tumbleweed of comb-over sitting on top. He was also wearing sunglasses in the dimly lit restaurant. At some point during lunch, aiming his sunglasses in my direction, he asked, "How yew doin'?"

If not for the slight Southern accent, I might not have remembered the moment.

That was it. My first glimpse of the iceberg from the deck of the Titanic.

POOL TIME

DENISE ANGELLE KINSLEY

I hear Kai's little person voice & wonder how to respond
to such Beauty & Light—pure Love / nephew with flippers
& blue trunks & little gashes or wounds here & there. I
wouldn't be surprised if he used the word "cicatrize" as
his little belly sticks out / childlike in the saltwater pool. I
attempt to swim laps in the overcast cool—thinking about
the imagination I have left. But soon we play / save all the
insects floating on top of the water. No Bees—just Dragon
fly, Fire fly, Horse fly, Mosquito & Flea. He wants to save all
of them & so the game begins / we become Super Heroes.
He tells me his name is to be Red Surfer and mine will
be Lisa—I want to say, "No, I'm Nisa because that's what
they call me in Mexico. Niça from water—from Zapotec."
But I don't, "O.K.," I say & look at his big frog appearance
underwater surrounded by concrete. The image of him
underwater: His face & arms & legs & his eyes look back at
me through buggley goggles / submarine portholes to his
soul / an Innocent baby surviving—exciting but scary at the
same time—just learning how to hold his breath, nicely. We
both come up for air, I say, "A jellyfish needs saving too!"
He says, "She or he?" I say, "What?" "*She* or *he*?" "Huh? . . .
Oh, *he*." It's a male jellyfish. I didn't understand the question

at first. Kai & me—his name also means water—saved a jellyfish from drowning; & we now believe it can breathe—just like all the other creatures in the water we want to save.

THE HOUSE

MEGHAN ANDERSON

The house was built to welcome the family during summers and weekend getaways. It sat near a lake that the children escaped to each morning, but they always returned collapsing their small tired bodies onto the porch swing, letting the house lull them into an afternoon nap. The adults busied their days fixing squeaky hinges and hanging new curtains, and although the house savored this attention, it patiently craved for the evening to take over. Bright lights would shine out of windows fading into the dark night, as sweet smells lingered by the warm stove, and laughter danced down the hall filling the once empty rooms. The house stood tall during these moments begging the crickets and stars to take notice. But the evenings always turned into sunny days and soon the family would begin packing. Taking from the house suitcases filled with clothes and blankets that once covered beds. Turning off lights and drawing the pale blue curtains closed. Wiping crumbs from the kitchen counter and sticky fingerprints from the handle on the screen door. It was then that the house dreaded the night knowing it would sit alone, surrounded by the sound of chattering crickets while beaming stars exposed dark rooms. And a cold wind would

blow through, sneaking in through small cracks, carrying
away the echo of laughter that was left dancing in the hall.

PRIMER

E. JACOBS BURROUGHS

In first grade, I slapped a girl across her face with a red, woolen scarf for calling me "high yella heifa."

Grandmother Nora, a slapper, would not have tolerated that behavior in me. It was at the end of the day, a chilly winter afternoon even inside the first-grade room. She stood behind me at the back of the dismissal line. Can't recall her name—only her bulky frame, beady eyes, ashy-dark coconut complexion, more maroon when her hand dropped from cupping her left cheek. The red, woolen scarf still clutched in my right fist. Coconut yelled, "Miss Wiyam, she hit me in mah face wit her scawf!" Never could pronounce Miss Williams' name right. The urge to slap her again churned inside.

While Coconut sobbed, the other first graders' bustling stopped. Their eyes froze on coconut and me at the back of the line...I watched Miss Williams approaching. Her fleshy upper arms, bosom, easy-swaying pocket hips maneuvered our room, careful not to bump into desks and kids. I liked that she was color unconscious. Dark-skinned, light skinned—didn't matter to her. It mattered to Grandmother, a former teacher, always calling dark complexioned folks "darkies." I never understood, since she was mahogany-toned.

Liked the way Miss Williams said my name, too, making me feel the way your mouth feels after that first bite of sweet potato pie—warm, creamy, unlike the salty taste in my mouth when my grandmother cracked out my name, as if snapping green beans. Miss Williams' smiling almond eyes had narrowed into disappointed when she finally reached me. "I'm going to have to call your grandmother, Evelyn." My "Yes, Ma'am," tasted like an iron crowbar.

At Grandmama's graveside service, twenty-three years later, my tears, salty icicles, I felt that red, woolen scarf slipping through my fingers.

HAUNTED

ESTELLE GILSON

1
Rome. I wish I could remember how old you were.
Eleven, twelve when we schlepped you and your brother
from church to church
Daddy liked architecture
perhaps too much
When we three waited on worn Roman corners
gelato shortened our time.
How many pilasters and pillars, braces and buttresses
How many cupolas, arches, vaults and domes did we see?
How many martyrs and saints, Christs and Marys?
The Pietà

2
Too weak to shave
Too distant on your white sheets
for me to do other than kiss your black bearded face,
you smiled when you said, "enough already" and I
smiled back.

I wish I could understand what you meant.

NONE THE LESS

J LONACK

kindness
likes to wear clouds
for shoes

and leap
over
  red bicycles.

but only
when
  No One
is paying attention

and the wind is busy
puppeteering trees

  .

THE ELEPHANT AND THE WOLF

JANET FOSTER

the elephant sipped
a long cool drink
before stepping in
to calm blue waters
with her lover, the wolf
who loved her more than meat
and draped her parched skin
with darkened moisture,
his own fur
now clean
from all past kills,
while a man in a plane
flew overhead
searching
for predator and prey
only finding
large flapping ears
enfolding
sharp jagged jaws,

the two embraced
in a sculpture of
trunk and torso
clay and pelt

BOY WHO FELL THROUGH TIME

ALEPHONSION DENG & JUDY A. BERNSTEIN

Chapter 1: Magic Power

Four ropey scars raking down my father's shoulders stretched and curled as he pulled his hoe through the hard earth. The midday sun beat down on the soil, the dried sorghum stalks, and us.

"More water, father?" I asked. That was my job, fetching the water he often needed.

My father, Deng, wore his scars with pride. When I was smaller, too young to understand it all, I'd heard pieces of how he got those badges of courage. My father had saved our village from a renegade lion.

I handed him the gourd of water. As he drank, a white streak made its way across the sky in the same path as the sun and moon, spreading its tail, slicing the blue in two. Strangest cloud I'd ever seen.

"Father, up there. What is that?"

"Alepho, that's the big bird."

"Where does it come from?"

My father pointed west. "Far away where the sun sets there is a huge lake. Only the big bird can cross it. On the other side of that lake is another land."

"Who lives in that land?"

"White people live there. They use magic power to control the big bird. That magic has even taken them to the moon."

"How did they get their magic power?"

"They went to school. They have education."

I was only four, but that story stuck with me. I wondered about white people, what they looked like, and their magic power that let them fly. I wanted that magic power too.

"Father, please tell me the story of the bad lion who gave you the scars."

"Tonight."

Tonight. He often promised that, but most nights he was too tired from working in the fields to entertain us kids with stories.

We lived in Southern Sudan, in a region called Bahr al Ghazal, which means river of the gazelle. My family called our small village of grass huts, Juol.

Our people, the Dinka, valued cows in many ways. We seldom ate cows, except on special celebrations. We used their milk to drink and make cheese. A man who owned many cows was considered rich. If a young man wanted to marry a strong girl who could cook, he needed two hundred cows to give to her family.

We grew grains. At harvest time, people filled the wheat and sorghum fields. Each person bent over, grabbed a fistful of grain, and cut off the tops. When they let go, the stalks swept back up into place. In the tall grain, you couldn't see the people, just bunches of grass going down and springing back up. The whole field moved with the rhythm of drums. I loved watching the grasses dance.

In Dinkaland, every part of the plant was used. The remnants of stalks and roots were dried and the women wove mats, baskets, and even roofs for our mud huts. They pounded the grain, cooked the food, and looked after the children.

I looked after the baby goats and cows, brought water to my father in the field, gathered firewood, and went to our neighbors for a small flame on a stick to light my mother's cooking fire. Girls fetched the water. The walk to the bore hole was long and carrying the full water pot back to the village was difficult.

When we weren't working, we played, chasing squirrels, rabbits and dik-diks, small antelopes. If ostriches were around, I stole their eggs. I had to watch out for the mother; she could kill a boy with a single kick. I could only carry one heavy egg at a time. My mother fed all of us kids—six boys and three girls—with just one ostrich egg.

The evening of the day I saw the big bird, my father called his children together around the fire.

"Tell us a story. Tell us a story." We chattered like a tree full of weaver birds. I hoped he remembered that I wanted to hear the story of the lion.

My father settled himself. We went silent. My father looked at each of us and said, "Our family has had a traditional covenant since the olden times of your great-grandfather."

Oh no, not traditions and covenants. I wanted the lion story, not lessons on how to live in the village. What was a covenant anyway?

"That covenant began one night when a pack of hyenas encountered an ailing male lion."

I sat up straight. Maybe this was the lion story and not about a member of the village.

"You see, the lion is the worst enemy of the hyena. Those hyenas circled that sick lion; they wanted this chance to destroy him."

He paused and looked at each of us who were as focused on him as prairie dogs on a honey badger.

"The lion knew he couldn't win this fight so he ran into your great-grandfather's house. Your great-grandfather chased away the hyenas and protected that sick lion. Early the next morning when he opened the door to let the lion leave the house and he offered a lamb to this wounded lion."

"He gave one of our lambs to a lion?"

"Yes, he did. Your great-grandfather was kind and also wise. His gift paid off. Later, when famine came, that lion killed an antelope and dragged it to your great-grandfather's house. This was the lion's way of showing his gratitude. Your great-grandfather came into friendship with the lion. Our family lineage has followed this partnership.

The lion does not harm our family animals. He protects them and our family members give the lion an animal to eat as a reward."

"But how did you get the scars?" I asked.

"When you were small boy, a lion began massacring our animals without eating them. This lion had broken our old covenant of friendship. Your uncle and I took a fat black male goat into the jungle and tied it to a tree. We hoped that with this gift to the lion, he would stop eating our family animals."

"Did the lion stop?"

"That goat cried day and night. But the lion refused our offering. After three days, I brought the goat home. The winter grasses were as high as my neck and I didn't see the lion shadowing me. I put the goat in the pen with the others and went to the domino tree to play with your uncles.

"The next thing I heard, a neighbor screamed, 'Help, the goats!' I ran for my spear. When I reached the pen, many of the goats lay dead. Others shivered with fear in the corner and threw away their dung. The lion had jumped from one to another like a silly kitten playing with toys.

"'Lock the children in the hut,' I told your mother. I called Dingmak to join me."

Dingmak was my oldest brother by my father's first wife.

"'Dingmak said, 'I don't think only two of us can fight a lion.' 'Son,' I told him, 'the rules have been broken. Quell your fear. I must kill this lion.'

"I took my ten light spears and the large harpoon for hippopotamus and tracked the lion's paw marks into the sorghum stalks. We split into three groups. Your uncle and brother and two neighbors. Each group tracked the lion in a different direction. Dingmak and I followed the paw prints through sorghum to a trench on the other side. When we reached the lip of the trench, there sat a big male lion. He had made his stand."

My father waited. A playful smile came across his face. We exploded like ripe mangos hitting the ground. "What happened?" "What did you do?"

My father cleared his throat. "I told Dingmak to step back. He was young and didn't have the strength or experience. Facing a lion needs fortitude and confidence to fight to the end."

I couldn't imagine how my brother felt seeing that crazy lion right there ready to throw him around like a lamb and try to kill my father. What would I have done?

"Holding all of the spears in my left hand." My father went down on his hands and knees before continuing his story. "I crawled forward along the rim. When I was right over the lion, I slowly pulled a light spear from my left hand and even more slowly pulled back with my right and stayed like that for a moment to not put the lion on guard." My father rose up and showed us his battle position. "I thrust that spear with my full strength. *Shhreeet.* The spear sliced the lion's left ear, stuck into his hip, and broke."

"Oh. Oh. What did the lion do?"

"I didn't want this fight. I didn't want to kill a lion. I hoped that spear would scare him and he would flee and leave our village in peace. But he didn't run. He crept up the embankment with his yellow eyes focused right on me. I rose to the crouching position with one knee on the ground. That is the only suitable way to battle the lion; he cannot knock your face into the dust or bite the back of your neck. I told Dingmak to call for help. But his mouth couldn't move. He'd been made voiceless by fear.

"The lion's tail twitched left and right, raising a cloud of dust. I took a second spear from my left hand. The lion crouched into the cat's posture to jump."

"What about the neighbors? Where were they?"

"They climbed the baobob tree. I aimed for the midpoint of the lion's head and threw the second spear. The lion was quick. He dodged the spear and at the same time charged up the side of the trench in two huge leaps. With my right hand I quickly pulled the big harpoon from my left and held it tight. The lion knocked me flat on my back. He was on me, heavy as three men, and his fore claws dug into my shoulders. All the spears scattered from my left hand over the grass. We stared into each other's eyes.

"I couldn't lose that harpoon. I clung to it with all my strength, but I couldn't raise my right arm with the lion's weight on my shoulders. The lion lifted up and opened his mouth wide to take my neck in his jaws. That would be my end. I looked into that mouth dripping slippery saliva. With my left hand now freed, I did the only thing I could. I plunged my hand into his mouth and grabbed that big pick tongue and twisted it with all my strength. The tongue folded and the lion couldn't bite down. He froze, somehow surprised. No one had grabbed his tongue before. With my right hand I moved that harpoon against his belly. His stomach concaved but the harpoon didn't pierce the skin. The lion tried to free his tongue. With all the strength of the right side of my body, I shoved the harpoon hard. This time it plunged into his stomach. I jerked my hand from his mouth and shoved him off me. He rolled down into the trench with the spear sticking out of his stomach.

"Your brother's voice worked then. 'Oh oo, Oh oo, he kill it. Dad killed the lion! Everybody come and see, haheee!'

"You all came out of the hut with your mother. The villagers arrived and stood over the dead lion and stabbed him with their spears saying, 'You deserve it. Deng sent you to your lion graveyard for messing with his animals.'

"The village men helped me up and splattered some water on my shoulders to clear the blood away. It was no use, the bleeding wouldn't stop. The lion's claws had torn me from my shoulders to my chest. That night they carried me on their shoulders to the town two hours from here. The clinic there transferred me to the big hospital in Wau."

Our mouths hung open, frozen like Dingmak.

"That was just the beginning of the lion war."

Chapter 2: The Lioness

"Am I deaf?"

"You're not deaf," my mother said. "When you were a small child you didn't listen. You put a stick in your ear and spun in a circle until you fell down on that stick."

"Kids say I'm deaf."

"Can you hear me?"

"Yes."

"Your other ear works."

My life in the village was wonderful except for that one problem. Many nights I couldn't sleep because of pain in my left ear. Pus ran from it, and it hurt as badly as the time a scorpion had stung my foot. My mother prepared medicine from special plants and put that into my ear. Still it never worked right. Kids teased me. "You don't hear many things, and your ear smells bad."

These teasings drove me away, so I often played with Achol who didn't say those mean things. We made cows and built houses of twigs. "I am the mother," she'd say, "and you are the father. You tend the cows, and I make the food." She cooked with sand, and we pretended to eat. Achol never teased me about my ear or that I was deaf. I protected Achol when we played, and she felt safe with me. We never fought.

One day a man came to us with a small black monkey. "This baby monkey lost its mother. You kids take care of it."

He set down the baby monkey and left. The little monkey trembled and looked sad. He was afraid of us.

"I'll bring him some milk," I said. I returned with the milk and placed the cup on the ground. The monkey looked at it, and his eyes grew big. He looked up at Achol and me.

"It's ok, little monkey. It's for you."

He put his hands on the cup and looked at us again as though surprised it was for him, and we weren't taking it from him.

"Drink the milk."

The monkey took a sip and looked up like a baby. He took another sip. After that the milk was gone quick as a mango falls from a tree.

The monkey thought we were his family. He rode on my shoulder and played with Achol and me. Sometimes he stole our little clay cows. When he grew too big to be on my shoulder, he walked with us. His baboon teeth grew, too. "That monkey will bite you," people said. They moved away from him. He never bit me. I loved that monkey.

At times, family members from other villages came to visit. My mother would introduce us. "Alepho, this is your aunt and this is your cousin." I was shy because I didn't know them. One cousin, Joseph, came often with his mother. Joseph was tall and strong and several years older. I looked forward to his visits. We ate food together. Afterward, I wanted to play with Joseph, but my older brother always took him away, leaving me behind. I was still the little guy.

My father was an important man. He settled disputes in many villages. Each time he traveled, he took one son with him. To be chosen was a great honor. My older brothers argued over who would be next but the arguing was wasted; my father was the only one who chose. Each time a son returned from a trip with my father, he held himself proudly, as if he'd been named chief.

For weeks we pestered and begged my father to finish the lion war story, but he was either too tired from work or gone. Finally one night he summoned us to the fire.

"Didn't the lion die?" I asked.

"Yes, the male lion died."

"Why did the lion war go on?"

"Do you remember when I was away at the hospital for a month?"

I didn't remember.

"The male lion had a mate. That lioness was enraged that her husband had been killed. Your mother took care of you children and our animals. The men from the neighboring village looked after her, and your older brothers helped with my duties and tended the goats and cows.

"One day your brother saw a lioness creep from bush to bush in broad daylight. He collected the animals back to the village and put them in their stable. Your mother locked all of you in the hut.

"That night the lioness came. She clawed at the latch of the house door. She crashed herself against it. Your mother took up the very same harpoon I'd used to kill her mate. Your mother made her voice deep and shouted like a man. But the lioness seemed to know that she was just a woman like her. Your mother stabbed the harpoon through the door, trying to drive that lioness away but she did not go away until the sun was above the trees."

I hadn't remembered anything about the male lion or my father being gone, but I remembered that. I'd never forget that lioness attacking our hut. We'd been so frightened. All of us screamed and cried, and our mother fought that lion all night.

"The next morning the village men came by to see what the lioness had done, and they made the door stronger. The next night and every night after that the lioness returned and patrolled the courtyard. She clawed at only your door and roared throughout the night. Your mother couldn't even sleep for fear the lioness might break the door if the harpoon wasn't stopping her. Every day the men escorted your mother to fetch water from the river or collect firewood to cook our dinner. Everyone in the village knew that the lioness was looking for revenge for the death of her mate. The village chief warned his henchmen not to let harm come to you while I was away."

My mother came out from the hut and stood in the doorway. She smiled at my father. She must have been listening too.

"I came home after three weeks hobbling with a big stick. That very same night, the lioness left the village and went back to the jungle darkness. But sometimes we still heard her roaring."

When my father finished the story, we rose to scatter to our huts for sleep.

My father said, "Alepho, come here."

I went to my father.

"Tomorrow you will come with me."

I couldn't believe it; my father had selected *me*. I was excited but nervous. I went to bed early, ready for the following day. Excitement kept me awake all night.

DUTIFUL DAUGHTER

JOAN GERSTEIN

High noon and muggy,
air as thick as putty.
Dogs lie on cool linoleum,
birds perch like statues.
No rustling bushes, crickets,
or people on the street.
This torpid backdrop, where
I find myself—just an ordinary
August day in Florida.

Armed with tranquilizers,
lots of distracting toys,
Alice B. Toklas brownies,
I visit my mother
who lives amid ugly condos,
endless strip malls and
a plethora of *early bird specials*.

One week, often only 6 days,
this annual visit will last a lifetime.
I stop at the kosher deli, order
Mom's favorites—stuffed cabbage,

bagels and lox, corned beef,
presents to deflect criticism.
I will fix what needs fixing,
run errands, shop, make calls.
We'll go to favored restaurants.

Conversation's the challenge.
Her interests, knowledge, friends
have shrunk but not her harsh
judgments or piercing tongue.
As a child I wished for a different
mother. Now I know people
don't change. Still, when we hug
good-bye, I feel her sigh for a moment
as if she wished she could be different.

CIGARETTE SISTER

TULLY S. REED

1974. Sloppy brown hippy purse, sans fringe, brought around front to rest on her right hip. My mother digs through it with delicate hands, fingernails ragged and chewed, seeking—her hands pushing through the contents until she finds it. Frantic, she pulls out a red leather cigarette pouch: snap closure at the top, homemade, leaf-prints burned into the flesh with a hot knife, the blackened spark wheel of a Bic lighter peaking out of a small pocket on the front like a charred marsupial.

Whoosh, out comes the lighter. Snap, divide, pinch—forefinger and thumb tease out the cigarette pack. *Virginia Slims, baby.* Flip, turn, tap. Two cigarettes emerge, one selected, the other rejected. (*Don't need you, yet.*) All items deftly managed by my mother's swift digits: case, lighter, pack, cigarette. One strap of her purse surrenders, jumps off the cliff of her shoulder. The other holds on with weakening resolve. Mother digs her elbow into the purse, holding it against her hip like a squirming child, just in case it tries to make a break for it. (*You're not going anywhere...*)

Cigarette thrust between her lips, wet and pretty, coral lipstick. Items rearranged quick like a magician so she can thumb the Bic into a flame. Her mouth puckers, sucking, fire applied to tobacco tip, glowing. She inhales, inhales. Leaf turns to ember turns to ash.

She inhales.

All at once my mother's face relaxes. Her shoulders sink slightly, both straps gone now, abandoning her. The purse tries to follow and is caught with a forearm that causes my mother to jerk slightly to one side. She leans against the wall of the Safeway. It's getting dark.

Mother inhales again, deeply. I exhale, slowly. *She'll be OK, now. So will I.*

I envy the cigarette, look up to it like the big sister I never had. It's a funny thought: *my Cig Sis.* Mother turns to her for comfort, and I'm both jealous and grateful. Slender and inviting, gently held, thoughtfully regarded—*Cig Sis* is unlike me in every way, it seems. It's not all good times for *Cig Sis,* though. Used up, a trail of ash at my mother's feet, she drops to the sidewalk and is ground to death by the sole of my mother's boot.

But still, I'm glad she's around—*my dear, reliable cigarette sister.* If she wasn't, it would be me instead of her.

BEFORE SHE DISAPPEARED

JOSEPH MILOSCH

I could say I was in this tourist city looking for art,
   but that isn't true.
I was looking for a poster for my niece as she was
   about to enter
the seventh grade. In the Black Door, I turned
   placards and came across
prints of Duchamp's *Nude Descending a Staircase # 2.*

I could say I thought about that famous poem about
   Duchamp's painting,
but I didn't. I could say that I thought how he drew
   from the futurists
or competed with a new invention—movies—to
   depict a woman
in motion as she took the stairs one step at a time. I
   didn't,

nor did I think of beauty as a contrast of light and
   dark. I don't mean
dark portrayed as an emotion but as color like the
   shadow that

cottonwoods cast along the banks of a desert river.
  Was it because
I was looking for a sentimental poster that the Nude
  touched me?

I bought a poster of a rainbow with unicorns and
  butterflies and
carried it through the streets of this place. As I
  walked, Duchamp's
Nude haunted me, and by evening it began to rain.
  Entering a basement
bistro, a young woman passed me on the steps.

As she ascended the stairs, the rain formed beads
  on her hair. Reaching
the top, she shook her head, spraying water. When
  the click of her high-
heeled boots became metallic on concrete, I saw her
  tan coat turn
transparent before she disappeared beneath the
  streetlights.

THE DAY WE FLED

KRISA BRUEMMER

Unlike most of the other stay-at-home moms, mine wasn't the type to volunteer at school or show up unannounced to help out or drop off snacks. Then one day I looked out of my fifth grade classroom's door and saw her standing there. She looked impeccably stylish in her tall pointy shoes and her skin-tight jeans that she had to pull up by the belt loops. My breath became raggedy as my suddenly pounding heart threatened to burst out of my throat.

Mrs. Delano continued to read aloud from "Redwall," my favorite book at that point. She was reading in a silly mouse voice when my mom walked in, her heels clicking loudly on the tile floor.

"Krisa, we're leaving! Get your stuff!" Mom said when I made eye contact.

My brain told my body to stand up and get out of there as fast as it could move, but as I looked around and caught the eyes of my classmates, every part of me froze. A boy I hated was snickering and pointing. The most popular girl in the room had her eyebrows raised, her lip snarled up in a way that let me know she couldn't wait to spread this scene around at recess. Everything seemed to slow down, and I felt like I was paralyzed underwater. Mrs. Delano was staring open-mouthed at my mother, and I wondered if the next thing that came out would be in mouse voice or human.

"Now!" Mom shouted, sending little white flecks from the foaming corners of her mouth onto a small desk in the front row. That foam was a sign of what my little brother Josh and I called "Ragwoman." Once the foam kicked in, we knew Ragwoman was going to be around for a while. The best thing to do was keep your head down and try not to draw attention to yourself. Being along for the ride was bad enough, but getting swept right up into the eye of the storm, well, that was the most dangerous place to be.

"Krisa's sick and she's goin' home," Mom said, glaring at Mrs. Delano. Her expression dared my teacher to try to tell her what to do or how to raise her kid.

My mom's face was quickly becoming red and furious, her eyes more wild by the second.

"Now Mrs. Gardner..." Mrs. Delano started.

"Don't you even start with me right now," my mom hissed.

Nervous laughter surrounded me as I stood up and began shoving stuff into my oversized backpack, trying to keep my eyes on the small gray speckles on the tiled floor instead of looking at my classmates. My hands were shaking and clumsy, and I left a scattering of dropped school supplies on the floor. As I walked across the front of the classroom toward the door, I could feel the other kids' eyes bearing down on me. Everything blurred.

"Listen. I parked the car in a *school buses only* spot and your little sister's out there alone with the car running, so I need you to hustle it up," my mom said, staring straight ahead, her angry, I-could-have-been-a-supermodel stride leaving me a few steps behind.

I could see the foam at the corners of her mouth building. Her face was shining with the exertion of her emotion, messing up her perfect makeup. She loved to talk about when she'd gone to modeling school at eighteen, where she'd learned how to apply eyeshadow "like the pros." But now her eyeshadow was smudged and there was mascara smeared across one of her temples and her cheek. I wondered if anyone back at modeling school had ever seen her looking like that.

"Why are you so mad?" I asked.

I already knew this had to be about Jim; the foaming mouth was almost always a symptom of her anger toward her boyfriend, my little sister Kaydi's dad. I felt pretty helpless around Ragwoman, but that didn't stop me from trying to figure out what was going on inside of her head. Usually all I could do was try to quiet Kaydi's crying by picking up her dropped teddy bear, or whisper to Josh that the screaming would hopefully be over soon.

"God damn it, Missy! I told you to be quiet but you just don't know what's good for you, do you?" my mom's voice rose, a fiery burst about to explode through the hallway. I flinched and my panic escalated. I had to get her outside fast. "I've got to deal with Jim out fucking whores all over the god-damned state, and here you are sassing me as if I don't have enough shit to worry about right now. I'm not gonna stand for any of his bullshit one minute longer though. I got a private detective on his ass this time, so now I've got proof that he's a slimy, no good, mother fucking weasel of a bastard."

"Oh my God Mom!" I interrupted, "Can you please be quiet until we get outside! That whole classroom just heard you."

"Don't you dare sass me, Missy Ann! You're cruisin' for a bruisin' with that smart mouth of yours," Mom yelled. "I don't give a shit if some bitch teacher hears me because she's probably been out fucking Jim too. You better zip those lips and hustle it up if you know what's good for you. Your sister could be abducted and halfway across the state by now because you can't just do what you're told and stop asking questions."

So even though I had known that Jim was a rotten scoundrel since the day I first laid eyes on his creepy smile and bloodshot eyes back when I was seven years old, I said nothing more and started to jog alongside my mom. My overloaded backpack bounced and I flinched a bit each time it landed, but I kept my mouth shut and sped up. I may not have known what was good for me, but I understood that it was my responsibility to protect the fourteen-month-old kid out in the *school buses only* lane.

Then Mom sent me into the lower elementary school alone to pick up my brother. Josh's teacher and the other staff at the school knew me. I'd spent three years there, before moving on to the upper elementary school, and the staff had learned that trusting me to sign my brother out was a lot easier than trying to follow any kind of protocol with our mom. I checked in at the office, handed Josh's teacher the misspelled note my mom had scribbled out in the car, and warned Josh on the way out that Ragwoman was on red alert status.

We went straight home to the trailer. Mom slammed the car into park in the driveway, jolting us all forward as she screeched on about Jim and his drinking and cheating on her with bar hags.

"Now you've got twenty minutes to pack your shit and then we're outta here."

Josh and I looked at each other, confused. We had just spent the whole drive home hearing about how Jim was gonna get it because Mom had proof he was a cheating bastard. Now we were leaving?

"We're getting away from his rotten lard ass for good, so take anything you really think you'll miss. Pack for Disneyland because that's where we're headed."

Disneyland?!? Our little sister Kaydi was far too young to understand the implications of what had just been said, but Josh and I didn't dare question the dream-come-true plan. We stared at each other in disbelief for a moment before blasting through the front door. Within our allocated twenty minutes, our warm weather clothes and personal treasures were packed, and we were on the road.

"This drive is gonna be total crap compared to our trips with Grandma and Grandpa," Josh complained before we even reached Seattle.

"Don't you use that language in front of me or you're gonna have another thing comin'," Mom shouted from the driver's seat. "Just shut up and play your Gameboy."

"I was just saying," Josh mumbled.

"Some kids don't get Gameboys and I'll throw yours out the window if you say another word. I don't have the patience right now to listen to your mouth. Stop being an ungrateful little shit."

* * * *

About fifteen hours later, I woke up to find us parked on the side of the road in the middle of the desert somewhere, nowhere near Disneyland. I tried to stretch out my cramped legs. It was pretty futile with Kaydi's massive car seat in the middle. Josh was crying and grumbling on the other side.

"You better be quiet or you'll wake up someone worse than me," I warned.

"I hate her!" Josh growled, his mouth all twisted up and shiny with his little kid snot and tears.

"I'm gonna give you a wedgie that makes your butt bleed if you wake mom up," I whispered loudly, pointing my balled up fist in his direction.

"I don't care if I wake her up. I don't care if I wake everybody up. I'm hungry and I'm tired and she told us we were going to Disneyland!"

I could see that Josh was starting to really lose it, so I pulled a lint-covered piece of candy out of my pocket and handed it to him with a forced, half smile.

He glared at it before slowly putting it in his mouth.

"She didn't even get us lunch or dinner," he said, slurping his words around the hard candy. "She didn't even get us a bed to sleep in."

"This is all Jim's fault," I said.

"She could have taken us to Disneyland at least," Josh whined, starting to cry again. "She could've at least let us go on one ride. She didn't have to drive right by like that!"

"We should've known we weren't going to Disneyland before we even left the island," I whispered. "It would have been too hard with Kaydi."

"Everything's always too hard with Kaydi," Josh said. "I'm sick of it!"

"I think we should just be thankful that Jim isn't here because his lard butt would be taking up all of the seats and stinking up this whole car," I said, sincerely thankful.

Josh giggled and snot shot down his chin.

"Where are we even going?" he whispered, finally making an effort to lower his voice.

"I have no idea."

We were about to find out.

SEEMS

KALEB COOK

She is a small stitch in her father's palm,
the fabric of a thousand blankets
on cold, dilapidated street curbs. She
is sixteen years old, a mother
inside her own womb. She tells me
it's like living inside of a dead body.
There is a bruised gash of flower petals
flaked and stuffed into her mouth. He tells her
to stay in her room when he fucks a woman
who doesn't look like his
dead mother. He is ashamed. But she
is a story he will tell to anyone willing
to see past him. She is still so small, her arms
and legs like sugar straws, a nest of curls
ribboned out of and over her head and eyes,
a heat-ridden garrison of hair, dry thoughts
and family photos. His heavy footfalls
mark time in the early lines of her face and hands.
He will never love my sister the way she deserves

to be loved. He does not see her. She is the Book
of Psalms on a shelf hidden behind stacks

of half-read Watchtower pamphlets,
a portrait of her two-year old face
taken at Sears in 2001, the blood
of his cock inside of a trophy case
inched in dust, dead skin. He has
seen what she will become for him,
what he will force through her lips. One day
she will know who he is through her children's
own eyes, but he does not tell her this.
Her chapped smile never sits in a room
with him longer than it takes to prove that she is
still there. By night the moon is strangled
in her lungs and she still holds her breath
long after spasms have given way
to a hollow cave in her throat. There is no story.
There is no other way to put it. She is
a floodgate, the labor of concrete walls
between a river, a small wilt of sunbeam
stealing through half closed blinds, something
like a pale world and not a star.

CHICAGO CONVENTION, 1968

CARRIE H DANIELSON

You wore a blue, green, and aqua striped tie, made of textile, not silk, the style in 1968. It enhanced your eyes— tortoise-shell, square glasses with big frames, hair, longer, trying to balance a law practice and the times. Your suit was dark gray, a light fabric, for the August heat. We stood next to the Cessna: 807 Whiskey Mike; I can hear you speaking its name into the radio, even now. My arm was in yours, holding on, wishing you would stay—ill at ease when you were gone. We smiled at the camera, me in my cut-off jean shorts, white Nehru shirt, and leather, hand-tooled sandals. The tilted rocks, the flatirons, loomed in the background, our roots dug deep in our mountain home. We were relaxed, even after my driving lesson…I drove the car into a hanger, denting both…you, exasperated but laughing, waving an apology to the managers there, them waving back, knowing you would fix it later. The photo over, you pulled me close (sharpened pencils and tobacco), and hugged me, longer than usual, saying, "Remember that I love you," as you turned to climb the wing. You dropped into the cockpit, started snapping switches—your eyes were sad; I saw it, a sadness swirling with the Colorado wind. I know now, that you were hiding something, hiding the ticking time bomb in your chest, 1968, no cure. I backed off when I heard the propeller engine chug. Headed to Chicago, a delegate for Eugene McCarthy, you relished a showdown vote against Viet Nam. You yelled, "We'll see to it that this war is over soon!" waved and slammed the door—your mysterious tears—felt mine coming, my throat thick. I watched as the plane growled down the runway, lifted gently and began to soar. You waggled the wings, and I waved back, loneliness as big as the sky. That's the last I ever saw you. At a hotel in the Windy City, your heart stopped—other guests thought you asleep—the nation watched the streets erupt against the war—the war that was to grind on year after year. So many lives were lost in those terrible jungles. I know one more it killed—one in a Chicago hotel, seated and alone, with a blue, green, and aqua striped tie.

SELECTED HISTORY OF PAPER

MARIANNE S. JOHNSON

What I have written,
I have written. Papyrus
nailed to a tree. Socrates,
retold. Parchment dried, unhaired,
limed skin. Koshered Torah.
Maps defined the world,
the jumping off place.
Gnarled monks, bent
with faith, their palms
inked with psalms.
A Chinese eunuch slaving
over wood pulp, birthing
typos and readership. Palimpsest,
print press, typeset, typewriter.
Tickety-tac, tickety-tac.
Shakespeare's margin scrawls
Da Vinci draws, scritchety-scratch,
the Vitruvian Man, xeroxed and faxed.
A declaration in steamy Philly—
Tom and his unalienable rights.
Origami flight. Rolled joints,
tokes, smokes and folded

boats. Leather binding epics
in the musk of libraries.
Charcoaled nipples brushed
down to pastel hips, poppies
in watercolor. Paper dolls in
perfect paper clothes. Paper cuts.
Crumpled scraps in the pockets,
in bathrooms, and subway cars,
newspaper rags our ragged edges.
Writs of habeus corpus, meaning
to have the body. Of literature.
Of language, of jazz blue notes.

HARPER'S DONELSON EXTRACT: HARPER, KATIE, AND FEATHERSTONE

SEAN KEVIN GABHANN

Monday, January 20th, 1862

Paducah, Kentucky

Jamie Harper sensed movement in the room even though he was not yet fully awake. Feeling no immediate threat, he let himself drop back to a deeper level of sleep, the way he learned to do during years in the Sioux Territory. When the girl climbed into the bed, she slid her naked leg over his thigh until her knee rested on his belly; she nestled her cold foot between his knees.

"Ready for another go, mister?"

Harper didn't open his eyes yet. He could smell the girl's woman-scent mixed with her perfume from the night before as her body warmed from its brief exposure to the January cold. She shivered when a gust of wind from the river penetrated the window frames and poked under a corner of the thick, warm quilt covering them.

She squeezed tight against him. He could feel the strong muscles of her arms, shoulders, and legs, now half on top of him. His body responded inevitably to her movement, and Harper was now wide awake, trying to recall where he was.

Paducah. He was in Paducah, Kentucky. Six weeks had passed since he had left Saint Louis to convalesce from his wounds at Belmont. His orders required him to report today. However, The First Iowa could wait an hour or so. The day had not yet begun.

He had paid twenty dollars to have the girl, the one they called Baby Red, for all night and that included her soft, warm bed as well as her companionship. He had heard that in the legitimate hotels in Paducah, the guests slept three to a bed with two or more on the floor.

Harper savored the feel of the girl's body against his, even though her hip and leg pressed down on the scars from his most recent wounds. After he reported to the battalion, he knew it would be a long time before he would find a woman's comforts again.

Through the girl's curtains, he could see the night beginning to yield to morning twilight—if there were any roosters left in town, they probably would start crowing shortly. That made the time about a half past six.

The light in the room shifted from black to fuzzy gray and Harper took in details of his surroundings, another habit from the trail. The growing light first revealed the white linen trim the girl used to give the room the comfortable feel of a home and not entirely a place of business. Cut lavender branches, now dried, stood in a vase on the dressing table, struggling to mask the residual smell of cigar smoke and stale whiskey from the saloon below.

She had replaced the blankets which still covered a few of the other second-story windows in the building with red and white flower-printed calico draperies. They gave the room some color and allowed for privacy when closed. The blankets now served as rugs in what he guessed was a failed attempt to combat the drafts and noise coming through the floorboards.

"Well come on, mister. Are you ready for me, yet?" She straddled Harper's hips, grinding down on them, but careful to keep the warm quilt draped around herself and her customer. Harper flexed and felt a twinge of pain in his rear from where a Rebel musket ball had peppered the muscle weeks earlier.

"I ain't never seen a man with them color eyes, sort of gray in the middle but with a brown circle around the edges. What country are you from?"

"My father was half Irish, half Spanish. My mother had green eyes." He smiled at her. "Like yours."

Although the girl stood only half a head shorter than Harper's six feet and taller than most women, Harper guessed her age at fifteen or so. But he really didn't want to know. She was older than his own daughter would have been and that was good enough.

Now, she hovered over Harper smiling wickedly and pinning his shoulders with her hands, her red hair hanging past his ears, mingling with his own shaggy, honey-colored hair.

Harper knew from the night before that red was her natural hair color; besides, the girl seemed too new at the trade to color her hair. The anticipation in her eyes and the movement of her hips gave the lie to the proprietor's promise of her virginity last night. He suspected virginity would return tonight if any new customers came into the saloon.

Sadly for Harper, his thirty-year-old body insisted only on using the chamber pot. As she moved against him, he battled with the decision to stay in the bed or to climb into the cold morning. Soon, biology decided for him and he gently rolled the girl to the side.

But before returning to the girl, he looked for his own belongings and saw the pile of dark uniform clothes outlined on the chair in front of the white muslin the girl used to skirt the small dressing table. His pack still lay next to the chair.

The girl held the quilt up tent-style, she reached between Harper's legs with her now-warm hand to get the man ready, then rolled back on top of him.

* * * *

Later, he dressed in the new uniform from St. Louis and gathered up the few belongings he used last night and this morning, surveying them all to make sure none had disappeared while he slept. He worked everything into his pack. The leather pouch lay loose on top of the rest of the contents—the special leather pouch. Inside were the only two things he had left from his life before he became a marshal besides Santee. He shifted it carefully along the sidewall so it wouldn't be crushed.

He knew the girl watched him. He took five dollars from his billfold. Crochet trimmed the frames of these two images, one showing a man and a woman, each with the stern, time-worn faces of people who worked in the sun to earn a hard living. The second showed the same woman seated with a younger version of the girl in a gingham dress standing tall beside her. The pictures and three dolls on a shelf above were the only indication of the girl's past life, before the war started.

There was no telling how much of his twenty dollars Bosley would give her. Staying here cost Harper a week's pay, but damn it, he would be comfortable on his final night of leave, so he left his last greenback, a fiver, under the image of the girl and the woman.

"What's your name, mister?" She sat up in the bed to watch when he shifted the daguerreotype. When he set it in place again, she pulled the quilt tight around her.

He thought for a moment.

"Lieutenant Andrew C. Ray, ma'am, Twelfth Illinois Volunteers." Poor Private Ray had died from bloody flux in Missouri the previous July and Harper had seen the flag of the Twelfth Illinois camped along the river the day before. He made it a rule never to give a hooker his real name.

Harper picked up his official issue, Hardee-style, black felt hat with the bugle badge in front identifying him as an infantry officer. He saw the numeral 1 above the bugle for First Iowa with a blank space above it where the company letter should go. He fingered the space and wondered what he had yet to do before the colonel would assign him to a company.

"Illinois, hunh. So am I!" She smoothed some wrinkles in the quilt. "I'm from near Cypressville, close by Shawneetown on the river."

"Which river is that, the Mississip' or the Ohi-ah?"

"My ma once told me we lived near the Ohi-ah River, but I know that Ohi-ah's a state, not a river."

Not the smartest of women, but she was pretty enough that he did not object to having a conversation. "Well, I'm from up in Chicago. Have you ever heard of that?"

"Of course I heard of Chicago." She pointed to the dressing screen. "Hand me them drawers hangin' on the screen."

Harper took the pantaloons from the pile of clothes draped over the dressing screen, without letting the party dress or petticoats fall to the floor. He handed them to the girl who struggled to put them on while staying within the warmth of the quilt.

"Y'all don't talk like someone from Chicago." The quilt fell from her shoulders revealing her small, girlish breasts, not more than large bumps on her chest. "When y'all comin' back, Mister Ray?" the girl asked.

Of course, she wanted him to return. He had been a good customer for her. "Can't really say, ya know. It depends on when the colonel lets me go." Harper's gaze shifted from her breasts to the etched muscles in her arms, shoulders, and chest. Those were the muscles of someone who had spent most of their life working on a farm.

"I like y'all, so's you won't keep me waiting too long, will you?"

Hookers always seemed to like Harper. Besides the extra money for his stay, she probably enjoyed having to entertain only one man last night. "It may take a while for me to save another twenty dollars." He lied. After he reported for duty, his position would require that he not be seen consorting with prostitutes or frequenting saloons, especially ones shared with enlisted men.

"That ain't true. Y'all bein' an officer and everythin'." She pulled the quilt back around her shoulders with a shiver. "Officers come into the saloon whenever they want."

"What did you do in Cypressville?"

"We worked our farm, jes' like everybody else. But after my ma died, my pa took to the bottle, so I did all of the work myself." That would explain the muscles. Harper found something attractive about a woman with muscles. He felt the strength in those arms and legs last night. The Sioux women were strong that way.

"Why don't ya go back to Cypressville and wait for me there?"

The girl's face clouded over and he knew he went too far.

"You know I cain't do that, mister! Mr. Bosley bought me fair and square from my pa. They'll both beat me if I run away." Her eyes filled with tears.

Things on the farm must have been desperate for a father to sell his daughter, especially a white woman. The father must have known how Bosley intended to employ the girl. Harper could guess the only way she would get away from this house was if someone bought up her bills to Bosley, and Bosley was not about to let that happen with his youngest and prettiest attraction.

The tears triggered Harper's sympathy for the girl's hopeless situation before he could catch himself. An image of Magda working in a saloon pushed into his brain, and he had to shake his head to force it away. Damn women and their damn tears.

"What's your name, girl? Your real name, not the one Bosley gave ya."

"Katie. Katie Malloy."

"How long ya been workin' here?"

"A few weeks. Since before Christmas time."

He needed to change the subject.

"Stop crying. At least ya have it pretty good here right now, eh." What did she think crying would help? There was nothing Harper could do to change things, even if he cared what happened to her. She obviously had not yet realized she would work for Franklin Bosley for a long time.

"I suppose you're right, mister." She used the sheet to dry her eyes. "Miss Loreena and Miss Eleanor take good care of us girls. And they says we're helping Mister Lincoln win the war by bein' nice to the soldiers."

That's a clever way to make her feel like less of a whore.

Harper was ready to leave. "Well good luck to ya, Katie Malloy."

"And to y'all, Lieutenant Ray. Be careful in the war."

With the war nearby, the girl-whore was a damn sight better off here than on some pig-farm in down-state Illinois. She'll probably have more money in a month than Harper could make in all of next year. And if it means she must lay back and spread her legs once or twice a night, well that's what the money was for.

He put on his overcoat and picked his hat up from the bed. Hefting the pack onto his right shoulder, he left without looking back at the girl.

* * * *

"Mornin', Lieutenant." Sergeant Joshua Featherstone greeted Harper when he came down the stairs into the saloon. "I thought I'd show ya the way, eh, since ya ain't never been to Paducah before."

Featherstone had been Harper's First Sergeant in the old Company K but the regiment reorganized after their initial, ninety-day enlistment. After the reorganization, Companies K and F merged into Company B while the regiment shrunk in size to a five-company battalion.

When Harper reached the bottom of the stairs, Featherstone lifted his pack from a chair and slung it over a single shoulder revealing hands permanently stained by tannin. "Ready?"

The sergeant had accompanied Harper for most of the trip back to the army. Harper spent his Christmas recovering at his brother's ranch near Sergeant's Bluff. The two soldiers discovered each other on the train to Dubuque and traveled together since.

Harper had come to trust Featherstone during the

time they served together in Company K. Harper was the company's first lieutenant, elected based on his reputation as a United States marshal, and Featherstone became the company's First Sergeant based on his role in the Fort Dodge militia. They had fought together through three campaigns in Missouri before Harper received his injuries at Belmont.

Now they addressed each other with the familiarity of men who had faced mortal danger together and came out alive. Rank still defined the differences in their responsibilities, but Harper held an unspoken, unabashed respect for Featherstone that he felt certain was mutual. Being two of the few remaining westerners in the battalion strengthened their bond.

The night chill had left frozen little peaks of mud in Market Street, but Harper and Featherstone walked on the duck boards bordering the building. The air smelled of wood smoke from hundreds of fireplaces being revived against the morning chill.

"How was your night?" Featherstone asked Harper with an insinuating smile.

"Probably better than yours."

"Ya smell like it. That girl's perfume is all over you, eh."

"Jealous?" Harper forced his legs to match the sergeant's pace, testing the strength of the muscles around his most recent wounds. Even at forty or so, Featherstone used the brisk walk of a man with important business. In spite of the sergeant's shorter stride, Harper felt pain in his left thigh and right buttock and struggled to keep the pace.

"I'm a married man." Featherstone reminded Harper. "And I appreciate ya lettin' me use your stateroom on the boat last night. I saw one of the hotels this mornin'—more like a pigsty for humans."

They passed the *European Hotel* on its narrow lot and Harper saw for himself an example of the over-crowded accommodations in the city. He congratulated himself on his choice of arrangements for the previous night. At the three-story brick mercantile on the corner, the pair turned away from the landing and up Broadway Street. Here the mud and gravel streets yielded to a macadamized road surface, and there was no need for wooden sidewalks.

The slanting rays of the morning sun threw the shadows of buildings and naked trees completely across the street but failed to deliver any warmth where the men walked. Their breath formed clouds of condensation in the still air. These dispersed when the men walked through them.

"Think there'll be trouble when we get back?" Featherstone broke the silence.

"We'll have to see."

"Those Company F fellows took it kinda hard that ya wanted to leave the Monroe boy behind."

"I know. I had a lot of time the last couple of months to think about that day. Maybe it would have been a mistake to leave him there if we weren't going to be surrounded." Harper knew he had made a mistake at Belmont, but he would not admit that the Featherstone or anyone else.

" 'Cept we were almost cut off from the landing and I needed to get as many as I could back to the boats." A pain shot into Harper's spine from the nearly healed wound in his thigh. "I'd probably do the same thing again if I needed to." That battle was in the past and whatever was to come, his actions at Belmont couldn't be changed. He would deal with the outcomes when they came.

"I understand why ya did it, but you'd best not be talkin' that way when we get back." Featherstone stepped around a mud puddle. "Things are gonna be hard enough for ya."

"A-yeah. 'Spect so."

They traveled a few steps before Featherstone broke into Harper's thoughts.

"They say the new commander wanted to make the boy his aide, ya know. Make him a lieutenant," Featherstone added. "It turns out Private Monroe was Colonel Monroe's son. The boy never told us."

"Yeah, I heard that too." Fate seemed to hate Harper.

"Now, I wish I couldda sent some of the old Company K boys to you instead. Wouldn't have been such a fuss then."

"Maybe. Maybe not." The men from Company K might have done what he ordered but leaving a friend behind might have been too much even for them.

"Well, we're all Company B men since re-enlistin' last August, so we'll have to learn to get along, eh."

In spite of his friendship with Featherstone, Harper wanted to change the subject. "Looks like the local folks don't seem to mind so much having Federal troops here."

He would learn the consequences of his actions at Belmont in due time.

"It ain't right, though, ya know."

"What ain't?"

Featherstone stopped and faced Harper. "It ain't right that you ain't in command of one of the companies. Ya need to do somethin' about it."

Harper knew better than to discuss the politics of the officers, especially with an enlisted man, even a trusted friend. "Well, I've tried already but Major Porter wants me on the staff and adjutant was the only position left."

"We've got a bunch of dandies runnin' Company B. We'd be a hell of a lot better off if you was the company commander. Them lieutenants don't listen to the sergeants, only to what Cap'n McKinsey says. It's harder'n hell just to keep from kickin' 'em in their fancy-pants butts sometimes."

At fifty-four years of age, McKinsey had held the captaincy of the Iowa City militia since Millard Fillmore was president and was well past the age when anyone would have expected him to lead his company to war. Fifteen years before, he may have been a dashing officer of dragoons. That officer now lay hidden under a hundred pounds of middle-aged fat. Harper believed that the man should be sent home. Instead, McKinsey retained command and drilled his men according to the school of 1843.

Harper walked again. Featherstone followed. Harper would not speak ill of any officer with any enlisted man, even Captain McKinsey. No matter what he believed personally.

"I'm doin' what I have to do, Sergeant. Doin' what I'm told."

They continued on the sidewalk a few more steps.

"Once campaignin' starts, there might be some openin's." Featherstone spoke what they both knew.

Harper chuckled. "You got anyone in mind you'd particularly like to see get killed?"

"Ya know it ain't like that." Featherstone bounded across another muddy puddle; Harper went around. "It's just that things happen in a battle and sometimes we need more officers—like for special assignments."

"If that happens, I'm probably in the best place get a special assignment." Harper stopped at the next corner to look down the blocks to his left and right. "It depends on what the new commanding officer wants to do."

"Yeah. I suppose so, but we need ya in a company. You're too good to be a pencil-pusher." Featherstone pointed to three large structures in the middle of the block on the left, their raw wood not yet turned gray. "Our boys built them stables. Good thing we got boys who know barn raisin'. Our enlisted men stay in the lofts above the horses."

They made their way across Chestnut Street to where the regimental flag of the First Iowa stood at the main entry to a white, two-story brick building. Above the doorway the name *Saint Mary's Academy* appeared, engraved into the stone lintel.

Featherstone followed Harper into through the door. "Good luck, Mister Harper."

Harper returned the salute of the guards as he and Featherstone entered the former school. For better or for worse, he was back in the army.

THE TROUBLE WITH WOLVES

MICHELLE FURTADO

1987 – Lake Catchacomba, Northern Ontario, Canada

This is the story Avo tells me as I braid her hair.

"Vo-voh, your Great Grandfather, was part wolf."

Sound seeps out of my pursed lips. I squeeze the comforting weight of the cord I have fashioned from her hair, feel its strands shift together while the great mass holds firm in my grasp before I fold it smooth between two other bundles of black and silver. My sound is an escape valve, a hot release of recognition. She sits in front and below me on the bed as I kneel behind her glossy head. She must take my sounds as agreement because she nods.

Continues, "Iberian wolf."

I know about sex. I have read all my father's science books on biology as well as his most recent articles on genetic engineering. I know about artificial insemination. I also know that Goa, now India, then Portugal in Vo-voh's time, would not have had the science for test tube babies. So there could be only one way to become part wolf. As the idea of bestiality floats to my mind, another sound escapes my lips. I clench my teeth. I try to constrain this bubble of hot shame lined with slippery incredulity. The little laugh sound slips out, bubbles up, froths and cascades out of me, so that I have to drop the braid and roll on the bed, holding my quaking sides. Avo turns. She levels her golden gaze at me. I still.

Like so much of us, our eyes match. I feel warmth resonate through me from her stare. I flop to my side. She pats my head.

She resumes: "He roved this way, that way. Through Portugal. Then over the sea to India." She holds one finger high. "He was a Butler on a Big Portuguese Ship. Very powerful."

Her eyes round. In them, I think I see a great moon, and in its light, the silhouette of a steamship. I wonder: Did Vo-voh prowl the ship the way a vampire would? Dracula at Sea? I push at the implications with my mind.

I can feel Avo's gaze on me. "He was a good man," she tells me, "He helped the nuns. Fell in love with your Great Grandmother. Saved her from that terrible convent school."

"Why was it terrible?"

"All those bloody Padres making babies in the tunnels. Shi! Terrible!"

I roll my eyes, "Avo! Are you sure? Priests are not allowed to make babies."

"Heh!" Avo makes the sound that means she knows what's what. She is matriarch of the sound of truth beyond the eloquence of words. "Your Great Grandfather took your Great Grandmother from that convent and made her a

Great Lady."

I ponder all that greatness. I know it funneled to Avo. But did I get some too? I lace my fingers through hers. Another match. Long, dark digits with elongated nail beds. I curl against her. She runs the fingers of her free hand through my hair.

"Did she tame him?"

Avo grunts again, "Tame? How can a wolf be tamed, tell me?"

"So what did she do? Wasn't she scared?"

"Heh. Never. Scared of her own husband?"

"Avo. Tell me. Tell me what she did to her wolf husband."

I feel the caress of her long nails as they line my scalp, then glide through my hair again and again. My eyes lull to the rhythm of her scratch. Outside our cottage, I hear my cricket lullaby. The smell of bonfire drifts to me through the open windows.

I have almost succumbed to the night when Avo finally speaks.

"She loved him, Lupe."

＊ ＊ ＊ ＊

San Diego, 2015

24-Hour Fitness. 5am. A picture pops onto my screen. My sister Georgia gazes at me while curled in a chair on a gnarled wooden dock atop a black glass lake, twirling a slender strand of hair in her fingers. Her eyes are glowing yellow—over exposed.

The effect jolts me back to Avo. My heart constricts. Avo has been dead for ten years. Yet her eyes call to me—penetrating further into my awareness than the heavy breath of strangers racing to nowhere on the machines beside me. In the fluorescent light of the gym I plod forward, but my gait has less conviction. My eyes rove over my dimming iPhone screen, until it succumbs to energy save mode. I'm left bereft.

The thought of Avo at Lake Catchacomba rises like an apparition in my mind. This time of year, the air will hug the lake so closely that I'll feel its warmth press against my skin. I think of my family, loud in the cabin in the woods. Raucous.

So unlike my husband.

* * * *

Jeffrey is on a call in his glass-encased office when I arrive at his law firm from the gym. I've seen women radiant in Lulu Lemon work out wear, but from the way Ali, his assistant, is averting his gaze, I suspect I'm not one of them. Jeffrey looks up, crumples his brow. I resist the urge to hurdle the desk to smooth back his furrow with my fingertips, trail kisses across his forehead. He is so suave in the European, tailored suit I bought him that I find myself grinning with glee, as I look him over. He rubs the back of his neck, setting loose one thick white curl from the rest of the flock, which has been gelled into compliance at the top of his head. There was a time when my too big grin would have blossomed a smile on his full, pensive mouth. But today he looks at me as he often does, with an expression I can't quite comprehend, and recedes inward. Snaps his eyes shut. Looks away.

"Lupe, what are you doing here?"

"Just thought I'd stop in." My grin is gone. "Thought I'd see if you'd be up for a trip to Toronto. Georgia sent me a picture of the lake—"

"Georgia."

The name billows out. Hangs suspended in the air between us. My impulsivity—arrive at law offices in tight workout wear, fly off to remote regions of Ontario—these are all given new perspective when viewed through the veil of this word. Georgia. She is the arbiter of all things wild in my family. Wears tailored shirts and Prada heels. Animal prints. She does civilized well.

If we go, she'll mitigate the experience. Keep Mom from peeling off her clothes and thundering, breasts barely contained in her hands, off the dock for a skinny dip. Keep Dad from gnashing his teeth at black bears foraging at the dump. The smoke screen of Georgia has sanctioned the entire trip already.

—As I knew it would. I smile my wolfish grin and arch my haunches a little higher as I sashay past Ali on my way out to book our trip.

* * * *

Toronto, 2015

Our rental car is neon yellow. My son Jacob loves it. He thinks a neon Tercel is the equivalent of a Nascar racer. He is nine. He has receded from the real world enough that his school principal suggests we test him for Autism Spectrum Disorder Services. He does not qualify. I am the only one not surprised.

Jacob loves this yellow car so much that he actually pauses in his pursuit of crushing fruit on his iPad long enough to whisper, "Zoom zoom." My Canadian niece and nephew are fluent in French. Jacob is fluent in Commercials. It serves him better as a language than one might think.

Jeffrey has not spoken to me since the arrival lounge at the airport. All because I had tethered Jacob to our luggage while I went to hunt for our second bag. I'd used the silk Hermes scarf Jeffrey had bought me. And Jacob had been so immersed in his iPad he'd not complained. Had Jeffrey used the restroom while he had sat alone on the airplane while I cared for Jacob in the row behind, or had he used the restroom upon vacating the airplane, before baggage claim, or had he even tamed his bladder, rather than disappearing at the exact moment the luggage came hurtling down the baggage chute, he would have been present to round up our bags himself, and this would not have been an issue. As it were, he'd sauntered up late. His two bags were already procured, his only son tied by a scarf to one. Jacob had pointed to his tethered wrist and piped,

"Connecting People. It's Style."

Jeffrey isn't fluent in Commercial. He didn't appreciate the double play of a Nokia slogan paired with one from Solex, the electric bike I'd been eyeing. As usual, the cleverness of my boy lingered just beyond Jeffrey's grasp. My husband, the Harvard J.D., had rubbed the back of his neck and searched the airport ceiling as if looking there for an answer to some conundrum.

Then he'd untied the scarf. "My son is not a dog."

* * * *

I stare, sullen, out of the neon car. I roll down the window and sniff the air. Musky odors of earth and animal underlie the dominant scent of grass. My nose tingles in anticipation. Something out there is calling to something in me.

I tilt my head to my son, wondering if I'm the only one who senses it. "Jake, you smell that?" Jacob doesn't look up. His gaze remains fixed on his iPad. "We are Farmers. Dum de dum dum dum dum dum," he intones. So I know he smells the country too. We are getting closer.

With only thirty minutes to go, Jacob vomits into our food bag. I hear it before I see it of course, since my eyes are watching the shimmy of the poplar leaves in the wind around me. But my ears are sharp. They are attuned to the sound of gagging boys. I turn in time to see Jacob drop the iPad and grab the bag of snacks we've picked up from Surati Sweet Mart. My nose flares in dismay as Jacob's gags give way to torrential spewing. Poor Jacob. Poor sweets. I can't quite figure out why scenery is still rolling by.

"Stop the car."

Jeffrey is staring straight ahead, still ignoring me.

In the back seat, Jacob moans. I feel the hair at the base of my neck begin to rise. Jeffrey's hand is on the gearshift when I place mine on top of it, dig my nails into his knuckles.

"Stop. The. Car."

With an exaggerated sigh from my husband, we roll to a stop outside a wooden gate. I survey the beams of wood. They are artificially 'weathered.' I wonder why amidst a forest, anyone would pay to have pressed wood barriers put up. Beyond the gate I glimpse a trash bin.

I lean back to my whimpering boy and whisper, "Honey, give me the bag. It's OK. We're almost there now. You can get out and get some fresh air."

Jacob extends the bag to me, its frothy contents sloshing a little on his wrist before I can tie it up. He wipes his wrist reflexively on his pant leg. I sigh.

His voice is small as I take the proffered bag: "When you care enough to send the very best," he says.

I give him the grin we share, all teeth and no lips, and exit the vehicle, barf bag in hand.

Just before I reach the gate, it opens. Out walks a squat man. He places his arm casually on the entrance to the gate and drawls, "We don't take your kind of trash here."

I start to notice how ugly he is. His isn't pleasantly plump. He is flaccid, his chin lost in the padded flesh that jiggles as he breathes. When his jowls move, a red mole on the mound that should be his chin shakes. I watch the mole in fascination. It harbors two long hairs. I get a little swept up in watching the chin hairs. I continue moving forward. He stiffens at my approach.

"You can't come in."

Not by the hair of your chinny chin chin, I think, watching the wagging bristles. I ponder the protrusions. Perhaps they are more intriguing because he has barely any hair atop his head. I catch myself—I'm being unkind. I take another step forward, offering him my free hand. His eyes dart to my gesture of benevolence and he makes a little noise at the back of his throat. *He is afraid,* I realize with surprise. I take in his pudgy fingers gripping hard on the entrance to the door. They are so white they are translucent. I can see the pink of his blood beneath them. My gaze shifts to what he is eyeing: my long, dark fingers. He shifts beady eyes to the car. Jacob, his chocolate skin radiant in the sun, is leaning against the car door.

"Take your trash away from here."

I don't wonder if this pig is talking about my son. I know he is. Immediately, I feel a distinct and primal urge to sink my incisors into his jiggling jowls. I want to tear him to pieces. But I don't. I hold back because my son is watching. A familiar tingle is creeping up through my shoulders. My hackles are rising. My arm rises with them, so that my free hand points into his face. I snarl in French—a language I know my son won't understand.

"*Cochon.*" (Pig.)

I have turned on my heel and am marching away when I full stop at his response: "*Ta mere suce des ours dans la foret.*" (Your mother sucks bears in the forest.)

I turn and hurl the barf bag at his head. It misses. But its contents spray onto the fake fence. I think it makes the pressed wood smell a little better. When I get back to the car, Jacob is wide eyed. Jeffrey is rubbing the back of his neck.

"Lupe. Did you really have to do that?" He asks me.

I can't speak. My chest is heaving. I am huffing and puffing and glaring at my ineffectual, monolingual husband. Nothing is right here. Behind me, I can hear the tut tutting of the piggy. I see Geoffrey look toward him with sympathy. My eyes water. I stamp my foot and growl. Jeffrey goes off to negotiate. I get into the car and scratch my hands against my jeans. I see Jeffrey peel some bills out of his pocket. I see him pay the piggy off. Pay him for my trouble.

* * * *

When we pull up at the cottage in Catchacomba, Georgia cocks her head, searches first Jeffrey's eyes, then mine, for an answer to our malcontent. Jacob finally detaches from his iPad. He races right by her, hollering like a hooligan at the sight of his cousins. Mom and Dad wait on the enclosed porch.

They squeeze me, and Mom says, "Tell me."

So I do. I tell them the whole story, from Jeffrey's ill-timed pee break to my throwing a barf bag on the fence. My parents howl with laughter. In my peripheral vision, I notice Georgia, standing to the side, a plate of steaks fresh off the grill in her hands. Her back is stiff. She gives my husband a pointed look. He follows her away from our rumpus, out to the other end of the cottage, to prepare our dinner.

Part of me longs for their detachment, but I'm brought back to my family's core with my mother's declaration: "Good on you, Lupe. You should have bitten his bum while you had him!" This sets off laughter like fireworks, brings the children hooting into the foray, pretending to stoop and bite each other's butts.

Jacob screeches and hollers the slogan for Cottonelle with each bite: "Looking out for the family. *Chomp*. Looking out for the family. *Chomp*."

* * * *

The mosquitos come out early in Catchacomba. They can eat a hapless visitor alive. But my family has summered here for years. I know how to dress appropriately. I'm in my black jeans, long sleeved hoodie, and Roots boots by the time the kids have flopped in front of the television. Hood up, I head out the door.

The moon beckons.

It rises like a great pearl above me. It seems to have been borne from this water—its iridescence pouring into the tributary river and out to the lake below. If I had a better voice, I'd sing its praises. I realize Lupe means River Wolf. So my song would be instinctive. But Jeffrey would not approve. I wander into the hush of the woods instead.

Moss kisses the feet of the tall conifers. Moist pine needles blanket the ground. I pad about mercifully anonymous in this space.

Voices prick the night. *Georgia and Mark,* I think. I can see their silhouettes. I thought my brother-in-law had been held up at work; his arrival sparks delight. I scamper toward the dock. By a tall spruce, I stop. I recognize the voices now, hear their words as clearly as if I were sitting beside them.

"Jeffrey—don't."

"I can't do this anymore. Seeing you makes me realize

I've been with the wrong person all along. She doesn't make any sense, Georgia. I just don't understand anything about her. I never have. Now I know I never will."

His flock of white curls tilts, spills forward in moonlight as Jeffrey dips to kiss my sister on the mouth. My boots dig into soft earth, propel me forward to spring on him without me registering the command. But something happens just as I reach the dock. My sister's hazel eyes flash golden in the moonlight. I hear a sharp crack as she slaps Jeffrey across the face. He is thrown off balance. I pounce. He teeters for a moment. Then he falls into smooth black water.

I'm surprised by the diminutiveness of the splash as he goes down. I would have expected more from a tall person who can't swim. Maybe it's because he doesn't fight. Until the very end, I think, he is loath to make waves.

Georgia grabs my hand as we peer into the water after him.

"I didn't mean it," she implores me.

Jeffrey flails. I can hear his awful gasps. I'm trying to figure out how to fish him out. All the while the words of Georgia spin in my head. I smell her. Mango body butter cream. *She didn't mean for him to fall in love with her. She had no choice.* She is intoxicating, my sister. Fresh. Sweet.

And she chose me over him.

I remove my shoes and socks, thinking I might need to jump in, then change my mind and lean over to grasp Jeffrey's flailing wrist. I figure he'll be an easy catch, but he surprises me. He yanks me hard. I belly flop forward—

shocked mouth clogging with cold water so fast that I can barely utter a sound. So this explains his quiet entry. Just as the thought occurs it's eclipsed by a second, urgent notion.

Survive.

Jeffrey grabs my head and pushes me under as leverage so he can break the surface to breathe. The water muffles the indignant cries of my sister, but I can still hear her, shouting at him to stop killing me.

He really is an idiot, I think as I sink.

I'm not dead yet. I descend below his grasp and feel the bottom of the lake squish beneath my toes. Something soft brushes against my ankle, rousing me. Up above, the moonlight shines. I see the dark form of Jeffrey, his motion cumbersome. I push off the bottom, surge up to gulp air and grab his pant leg, then push as hard as my arms and lungs can take me, to Georgia. I release him to her, but he doesn't understand. He shoves me under again. I bite his hand, then grab it and place it firmly on the knotted, driftwood dock, gasping and spitting lake water as I do so.

Take him from me, I think. Then I push off.

Something ruptures deep within me. From that place I feel warmth rise. Hot shame lined with slippery incredulity. It bubbles up. I drift on my back and let it buoy my body. I shake with laughter. Tears, warm tributaries from this deep well inside me, slip into the cool water cradling me. Strange release.

"Lupe. Are you ok?" Georgia's voice snaps at me in the wind.

I should tell her I'm fine. My voice sounds floaty as it

drifts out of me. "I'm free," it says instead. I grin, recognizing the sound of truth beyond the eloquence of words. "Hey. Avo said we have wolf blood. Did you know?"

I feel my sister's gaze tender on me in the dark. Beside her, Jeffrey hunches.

"Jeffrey," I call. He half turns. "You should have loved me," I say.

The only answer I get is the solitary slap of his wet shoes on the path back to the cottage. Georgia remains curled on the dock, with me.

* * * *

I drift backward into the cold embrace of the lake. Moon water laps over my muscles. I take some into my mouth. It tastes of life below the surface—that dark and murky space that's matched by something inside me.

UTAH

NANCY LEMKE

On the barren Utah prairie, an abandoned house
leans drunkenly in the wind,
bits of past lives scattered in the weeds—
broken bicycle, rusted tools,
an old car on jacks.
Inside, a hand-knit sweater, yellowed and stiff
on the dusty floor
next to a pair of boots
patiently holding the shape of their owner's feet.

There is no one to ask about the woman
who put up the flowered wallpaper,
or the man whose bunions
left their mark in the boots.
No one here can say whose
grip is worn into the
handles of the tools,
or whether they were held like weapons
or trusted friends.

Just a long-dead sheep,
trapped in the house,
terrible eye sockets
staring silently out the window.

UP

RON SALISBURY

In his apartment, he has screwed hooks in the walls, strung cables from side to side in order to move from room to room without touching the floor. The stove is hung from the ceiling, likewise the bed, shoe rack, book shelves, TV and easy chair. He crouches on a mesh floor in the shower, the toilet is located at the top of a tall corrugated culvert pipe. He lays across the network of cables, reaches down and pets the dog who lives on the floor. The floor is the other world, his is up here.

)

CICADA'S CHAOTIC DANCE

RAVINDER SANGHA

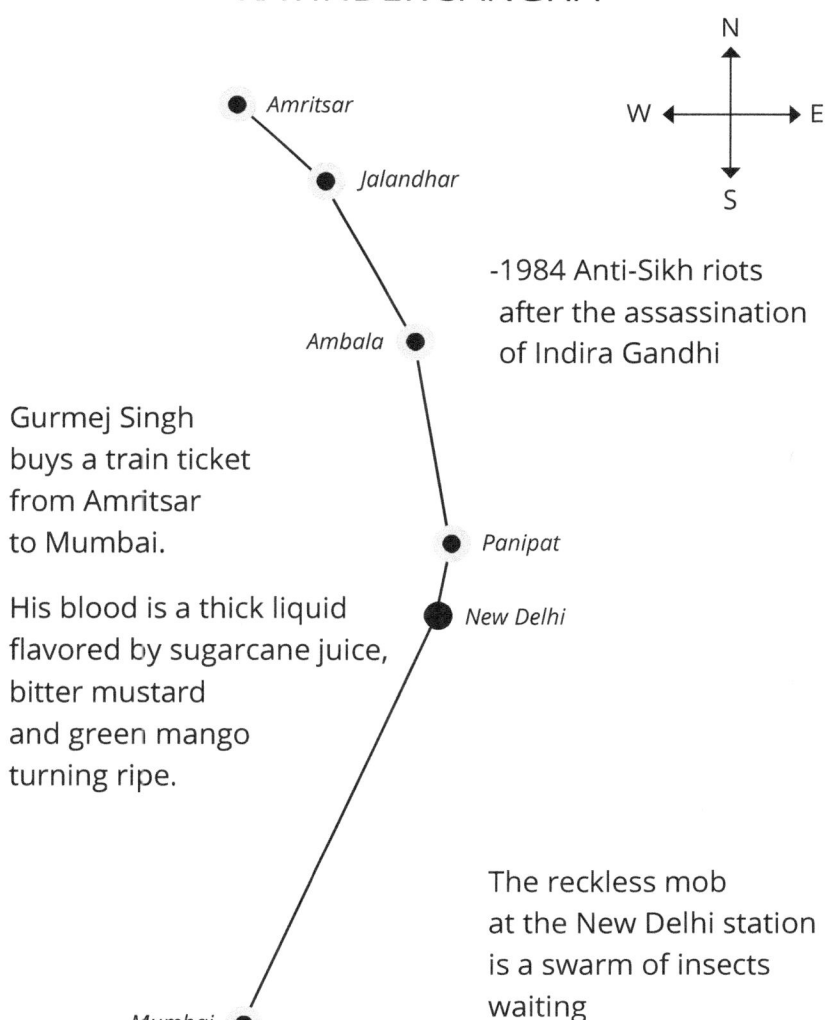

N

W ← ↕ → E

S

-1984 Anti-Sikh riots
after the assassination
of Indira Gandhi

Amritsar

Jalandhar

Ambala

Gurmej Singh
buys a train ticket
from Amritsar
to Mumbai.

His blood is a thick liquid
flavored by sugarcane juice,
bitter mustard
and green mango
turning ripe.

Panipat

New Delhi

The reckless mob
at the New Delhi station
is a swarm of insects
waiting

Mumbai

At the Jalandhar station
Gurmej looks at vendors
selling chai in clay cups
that can be thrown away,
becoming dust
that no one will notice.

           The Cicada carries
           in its thorax
           music that pours
           on the lips
           of night air.
           Cicada also cuts slits
           in young twigs.

At the Ambala station
coolies are breaking
their backs
carrying luggage
that comes
and comes.

     The hawk moth called
     Death's head
     carries on its yellow-beige
     wings
     imprint of galaxies
     as if it can fly the universe
     on its wings,
     but today

it will expose
the human skull mark
on its thorax,
symbol of danger.

At the Panipat station
a thin man sells
stone gods and goddesses
with flutes and snakes,
vermillion and ashes.

The Praying mantis
folds its arms
as if praying to its god.
Today it will use its
forelegs
with spikes
and apical claws
to catch and hold its
prey
securely.

And the train keeps
hurtling
and hurtling
towards
New Delhi.

GOOD OL' BOYS

SARAH Z. SLEEPER

My father lived a second life in the stories of Wolfe, Hemingway and Kerouac—the electric ones, the war ones, the love ones, the drug-and-sex ones, the smart ones, the art ones, the sparse ones, the exclamatory ones, the run-on ones—and he told me so, so, so, so, so, so, so, so, so and so many times, and he mixed them together with his own stream-of-consciousness New Journalism-version of the late '50s, when his life was better than best, all golden and glowing and fruit-ripe and he slept in vineyards in France and learned to love Châteauneuf-du-Pape that he crammed down his throat and mine. I turned away from flak-jacket-and-guns Papa, free-love-and-drugs Jack, and natty, smarty move-to-New-Yorker Tom. Dad wanted to live those lives, not be tied up and down in Lake Forest, on the wrong side of the editorial wall at the *Sun Times* where poetry wasn't the currency and money was. Dad tried, with summers at Ernie's abandoned Walloon, pitiful Midwest road trips, and old fashioneds at the Algonquin. I couldn't make it through an English degree without reading *A Farewell to Arms* and I couldn't claim myself as a writer if I didn't know *On the Road* and *The Right Stuff*. (If I read with a concrete heart did the words enter?) When my father died, I found a laminated card hidden in his wallet. It said, "Do not stand at my grave and weep," but I wept anyway for all that he had wanted to be and wasn't and for my stubborn slowness in knowing the man he was in full. Then I moved his library into mine. Now his lost dreams live with my inspirations, and Wolfe, Hemingway and Kerouac cohabitate and comingle with Fitzgerald, Nabokov, Roy, Munro, Marquez, and Erdrich. And my heart is no longer stone; it's a golden and glowing fruit-ripe ball of love for my father and his heroes. I've read all three of those good ol' boys from cover to cover and their words came all the way in.

The ekphrastic poem above, "Good Ol' Boys," was inspired by a painting of Tom Wolfe.

© Everett Raymond Kinstler, Portrait of Tom Wolfe, 1987. Oil on canvas.

MESSY THINGS

JUDY GERACI

September 1965, and every Tuesday it's the same routine. I walk home from Saguaro Elementary, stomp my feet on the carport mat to shake off the dust, and trudge through the kitchen door. Mom stops her ironing to tell me to wash hands and get my snack. I don't like cream cheese and grape jelly in a folded piece of Roman Meal bread, but that's what Mom hands me as I follow her down the hall. She's got the ironing board, the clothes basket, and a bottle of Magic Sizing set up in the corner of their bedroom. I sit on the rug, chewing the sweet, gummy-grainy concoction while she sprays and presses. Julia Childs is on TV, a small black and white box with rabbit ears (the TV, not Julia). Even without color TV, somehow it's clear that she's wearing orange today: orange lipstick and an orange smock of some type. How does the eye discern orange among the shades of grey? A mystery, but true, the same way it was always obvious that Lucille Ball was a redhead.

But back to Julia. She looks like a man in a lady's dress, so tall and lumbering, with oddly coifed hair and that orange lipstick just a little off. But never mind, because she is doing something wonderful with a chicken.

"Big bottles of red wine," she says and laughs a high, abrupt falsetto that adds to the drag queen effect. But never mind again, because the process is gripping. Mom never cooked like this. This is no ground beef and rice casserole made in the pressure cooker with frozen chopped broccoli and a heavy topping of oily cheddar. There is no ground beef. There is never ground beef. This was coke-ah-veen, or however you said it. Chicken with wine. And she was stuffing it with all kinds of herbs and spices, the likes of which had never been seen within a hundred square miles of my cinderblock house.

Eyes glued to the television, I learn that lemon juice does not come from a plastic squeeze Realemon and garlic is not a grainy bitter powder shaken from a jar, but a bulb that grows out of the ground. I watch, while the crockpot bubbles in the kitchen with a disk-like meatloaf smothered in ketchup and crowned with a green pepper ringlet. While Mom hovers over the ironing board working through a stack of shirts, Julia's sharp, high laugh fills the bedroom again, pouring out of the small class cage where she works. Elbows covered in chicken fat, garlic and God-knows-what-else, her arm is halfway up a chicken orifice, like some kind of primitive birth scene. Then I hear her say something on network television—without missing a beat or blinking an eye—in front of my mother and everyone else on the four p.m. circuit.

"It's really quite disgusting," she says, "but then so many pleasurable things are, aren't they?"

I laugh with her, not quite sure what she means but sensing in the undertone that she has just spilled the secret of the universe. I scrape a finger against the roof of my mouth to pry off the starchy muck that's stuck there. And out of the corner of my eye, I see the casserole queen as she presses down on the corner of a collar, ironing out every last wrinkle on the lapel, making it smooth, unmessy, and perfect.

BARREN BRANCHES

LAURIE RICHARDS

"To sin by silence when we should protest makes cowards out of men."

–Ella Wheeler Wilcox

Chapter One

After the drought started, our parched fields rose as clouds, thick and blinding. The wind scratched at the earth's skin, and I hoped that fertile land lay beneath. But each time the wind scratched, it exposed only sterile dirt, and each time, my parents increased their prayers. After three years of failed crops, they still believed God would someday bless Kansas farms with a harvest.

I didn't.

On a Sunday morning, I stared out our kitchen window at the haze. "Is it too much to ask to see dew, or even snow? Anything, other than brown air creeping around?"

"Can't expect dew in November," Dad said. He stood near the table, sniffing the biscuits Mom had just set down. Not even the biscuits' enticing aroma changed my mood.

"I haven't seen any dew since this damn drought started," I said.

Mom swatted my behind. "Language, Sarah."

I bobbed my head, but couldn't resist another stab at weather-hating. "Raise your hand if you'd like to damn this dust to hell."

With one hand in the air, Lily pulled off a piece of biscuit with the other and popped it into her mouth.

Dad shook a finger at me. "God'll send rain when he's ready."

Mom wasn't one to shake fingers; she shook her head. "I don't curse the dust, Sarah. It carries every step the pioneers took. And traces of buffalos thundering across the land even before there were farmers." She pointed toward our field and its stunted wheat stalks. "Dust shapes the soul of Kansas and yours too."

"So I'm only a brown cloud at heart?"

She gave me the lop-sided grin that said she wouldn't take time to lift both sides of her mouth. "Where's your poetic soul?"

I pointed to the sky. "Blown away."

"You inherited your father's no-nonsense streak," she said. "You're skinny, but that streak is wide." Then she pulled her apron toward her face and covered her mouth to cough. I suppressed the urge to pat her back because she didn't like any fussing.

"Even if dust shapes the whole country," I said, "it doesn't have the right to stick in your lungs."

She bent over. I put my arm around her, and she let me hold her while she coughed. When her lungs settled, she patted my hand and eased away from my hug. "My cough's not so bad this morning," she said, but her usually mellow voice grated like steel wool scraping our skillet.

"Not so bad as what?" Lily said.

"Every cell in your throat is screaming for air," I said.

She picked up the spoon from a pot of simmering oats and didn't look my way when she spoke. "You're spouting biology? I thought we finished that." The night before she had helped me prepare a lesson plan. Images of cells and genes still whirled in my head because I hadn't quite figured out how I'd get the facts across to my students. "Stop fretting," she said. "You'll do fine." She nodded toward the table, her way of asking me to sit down.

She touched the thick bun at the back of her neck and then wiped her hand across her apron, its gingham cloth so faded the squares had lost their corners. Dad held the kitchen door open and thwacked his boots against the frame. The dim light thrown by the kerosene lamp showed dust motes floating through the kitchen. Mom stopped ladling porridge and pointed the spoon at him.

"Make up your mind, Cal. Inside or out. I just scrubbed this floor yesterday."

"I have to say, Rachel, that floor's nothing more than slivers stuck in grit."

She plunked the spoon back into the kettle. "When I'm ready to call it quits on keeping this house clean, I'll let you all know."

Despite his grumbling, he made a great show of pushing the air outside before he closed the door. He squeezed Mom's shoulder as he sat down to tackle a bowl of porridge. "You ain't no quitter," he said and kissed her cheek.

"Oh, you." She grinned her loppy grin.

Dad was right about the floor. Try as Mom might, we hadn't enjoyed a clean house since the drought started and wheat fields rose up and blanketed Kansas. But if Mom gave in to a dirty floor, who knows what else she'd give in to. Fighting dust was breakfast, dinner and supper to her. With apple pie thrown in. Of course, since the drought started killing our crops, we hadn't baked pies because we couldn't afford apples.

I had followed Lily downstairs by just a few minutes, but she'd already finished breakfast. Her chair screeched against the floor as she rose from the table. "See you outside, sleepy," she said with a wink at me—a reminder of the promise I'd made to her. I didn't need a reminder, but I regretted the promise. If the land was riling up, Lily shouldn't be sneaking off.

She grabbed her mackinaw from a hook near the door and put it on. Mom set the kettle on the stove and stepped over to help with the buttons.

"I'm twenty," Lily said. "I know how to button my jacket, Mother."

Mom tucked a curly wisp of Lily's blonde hair behind her ears. "Almost twenty," she said. She pulled a red bandana from the mackinaw's pocket and held it up. "Wear it. You don't have to be glamorous for chores."

Lily allowed a small frown to escape, but she grabbed the bandana. She paused at the door. "You ready, Sarah?" I expected her to start toe tapping any second. She looked way too eager for someone supposed to be heading out for back-breaking chores.

The Tin Roof was closed on Sundays, and Lily wouldn't be waiting on people who still had money to spend. I wouldn't be at work either. Haywarden County would gather in churches to observe the Sabbath. *Everyone* did not include our father. "I can work and pray at the same time," he'd say, "and God won't mind." Sunday work on Irv Dennison's eight hundred acres was the only way Dad kept food on our table. So one day a week, Lily and I took on his chores. We picked rusted stalks from the hay and made sure weeds didn't steal what little water we had for the sickly wheat.

I gulped my porridge, swallowed without chewing, and hoped the dust bits didn't cling to my throat.

"Don't eat so fast," Mom said. "The chores will still be there. I'll help outside when I'm finished here."

Mom's intentions were always good, but she barely got the offer out before her lungs were angry again.

I moved to the sink and cranked the pump. A thin stream of water hit the tin basin. The plinks punctuated Mom's hacking as she held her ribs. We stared at her. She straightened herself, wiped her eyes. "You all stop dawdling."

Dad finished the few bites he limited to himself, as if his bones would splinter with a decent breakfast inside him. He didn't look scrawny, though. He looked tough and sinewy. He moved past Lily toward the door, gripped the knob and glanced back at Mom.

"Go on, Cal," she said. "You know what Irv's like if you're late."

"He's like nothing," Dad said. "He's got that soft spot for you and yours."

Mom was wiping crumbs off the table, but she winked at me. She had persuaded Dennison's grandson to go off to college, the same way she'd been encouraging Lily and me. I winked back before I scraped bits of porridge into the slop bucket under the sink.

"Leave the dishes, Sarah," she said. "If you and your sister are going to take on your father's chores I can manage cleaning my own kitchen."

Through the window above the sink, I watched my father mount Nimrod, whose ancient legs shivered as Dad settled in the saddle. They rode off in the dust clouds from Nimrod's hoofs.

When I was young and a minister preached about the Trinity, the man sitting at the right hand of God had my father's face—black eyebrows meeting above the bridge of the Mason nose, a thin, long nose. I had inherited that nose, as well as his dark hair and eyes. He used to tuck us in with a pat on the forehead and a fatherly command, "Be perfect as the Lord God is perfect. Matthew five, forty-eight." Perfection didn't come easy, but Dad said we had to try. I trusted him to let me know if I strayed, and I trusted Mom to keep it secret when I did.

As crop after crop failed, Lily's faith evolved into a

hunger to escape. She performed farm chores with the stiff-jawed determination of a daughter too loving to tell her parents that the constantly-shifting soil acted like sandpaper, slowly grinding down the rough edges of her hope. Once, she said to me, "Kansas will always be nothing but dirt. Let's head to California." She had waved her hand toward the night sky. "See that star? We'll hitch a ride." She was being melodramatic. It was too cloudy to see stars.

I wasn't about to leave Kansas because my father was determined to make it through, and Mom fought for whatever he wanted. At the last failed harvest, he held a rusted stalk of wheat in his hands and said, "We're being tested, and we can stand it." I didn't think about whether I could stand the test or not. I thought about how miserable I'd be without my mom. She was the dreamer, like her plan of college for me, and I hitched a ride on the stars she saw.

Who knew how my parents could hold fast to their faith in the Lord? We had stopped attending church because we couldn't tithe. Dad's pride wouldn't let him take when he couldn't give, but Sunday nights he held his own services. He'd pat the Bible and preach his version of Armageddon. "Disasters will pile up, and only believers will rise in the rapture."

Mom would nod and add, "Everyone left behind will suffer tribulations."

Surely her poetic genes made her blind. Wasn't everyone in Kansas and beyond already suffering tribulations, starting with the dust storms and the depression throwing so many out of work?

Lily and I didn't believe this was the end of the world,

but we usually listened out of respect. The way Dad saw it, we'd be raptured as a family. We were supposed to find each other in time for the main event, hold hands and rise together. I once whispered to Lily, "Like a clutch of balloons."

He heard and pointed a skinny finger toward me. "Even if the land is torn apart, a good family can go on if they're together." He opened the Bible as if searching for a pithy phrase to back him up.

"We're a small one, but a good one," Mom added. Big families went along with her big dreams. "If I had ten more like you two," she said, "the world would be lucky."

"Yeah, but would our politicians agree with you?" Dad said. He always thought black when it came to politicians, but I had no idea what he meant, and Mom must've seen my blank look.

"Kansas doesn't want some women to have babies," she said.

I scrunched up my face. "Why not?"

She patted her bun. "Some won't make good mothers."

"Who decides that?"

Dad looked up from his bible. "The people running this state pretty much do what they want with poor folk, and we're too busy scratching for food to fight back."

Mom glared at him. "Some women," she said, "shouldn't pass their genes on to babies."

"Like Dimwit Garner?" Lily asked. The Garners and their daughter Dimity were regular customers at the Tin Roof.

Dimity shuffled in by herself from time to time, and the Garners always had to be fetched because she didn't know how to shuffle out and go back home.

"That's cruel," Mom said. "Stop calling her that." Lily mumbled an apology. Then Mom shrugged. "Yes, like Dimity. And some others." She smiled. "Don't you two worry, though. You have Mason genes. Just what Kansas needs."

"Nothing wrong with our Connor genes, Mom," I said.

"Yeah, right," Lily had said in her how-bored-can-you-get tone. In a whisper so that our parents wouldn't hear, she added, "Nothing wrong moving the Mason genes to California, either." I worried about her can't-wait-to-get-out-of-here moods, but I didn't share my worry with Mom or Dad. They had enough problems.

After Dad rode off on Nimrod that morning, Lily left the kitchen without so much as a wave to our mother. Mom came to me at the door and pretended to smooth a loose strand behind my ear. I didn't have any blonde curl escaping like Lily. I wore my dull, brown hair the same as Mom did—in a tightly-wound bun, hoping to keep dust out—and it couldn't have been more uncurly. But Mom was democratic. A tuck for Lily, a tuck for me. She pulled a bandana from her apron pocket and held it before my face, with a grin as wide as if it had started raining. "What are you and Lily up to?" she said.

Should I have used the brains I'd been born with and worried her? Lily's going off to town. I drew my brows together, took the cloth and tied it like a robber's mask as I shook my head. The moment passed in a silence as good as a lie.

* * * *

Chapter Two

So Lily was going to Hayward, and I was stuck with all the chores—my own doing. Outside, I took stock of the farm with a hand visored across my eyes. The rope lines Dad had strung months before were still tight. In a duster, we followed them to get from one place to another—porch to barn to field to windmill to outhouse, back to porch. On the other side of the house, he'd strung ropes between the coop and garden, back to porch. Dad made Lily and I practice those routes time and again with bandanas across our eyes and without clinging to those swaying ropes so that we'd find the house even if they broke.

Plumes of dust floated through the yard and stretched across the horizon, dragging odors of musty hay and chicken droppings with them. Settled sand formed high dunes against the barn. From a barren branch of the cottonwood beside the house, six crows squawked. A dozen others harped at me from the rope connecting the porch and barn, the normal iridescence of their feathers hidden by dusty air. The pests in our county had bred themselves into the thousands. We received our share of government-issued twelve-gauge ammo so we could shoot on sight. Dad had taken out dozens of the birds. I never tried, but I would if too many infested our fields.

The harpies lifted off together, landed on the barn roof and scolded me. I drew a bead on them with my finger. "Quiet or I'll get the shotgun."

Maybe I shouldn't have been so unfriendly.

Near the trough, Beezer yapped at dust devils like an

idiot. The mutt circled around them as if that was his job and he was going to do it come hell...or at least until he spotted Lily leaving the barn. He beelined toward her and pawed at her skirt–her good skirt, not the raggedy one she wore for chores. She jumped back and shooed him, so he turned to me. With a snap of my fingers, he calmed down and followed me to the hen house, a coop that was collapsing more with each brisk breeze. Some day just one more fleck of dust would topple it for good, no matter how many times Dad shored it up.

Lily headed toward the county road. Two brown clouds joined and surrounded her as if trying to carry her along in the breeze. Most likely she wouldn't hear me above the wind and through my bandana, but I called out, "It's getting worse."

She was a slim, dim figure inside the dust, but she wasn't wearing a stupid mask like I was, and her voice carried. "Back tonight."

A little dust storm wouldn't stop Lily.

I lifted the bandana and cupped my mouth. "Don't go."

Dad's orders. He often told us, when the storms first started–and Lily must've heard him as clearly as I did—if a duster strikes, get in the house.

Most families holed up inside their storm cellars when a blizzard hit, but during the last one, four of the Kinkers suffocated when they couldn't lift the door as their cellar filled with sand. Dad had joined in the work to clear away the dune covering the cellar. Little Dottie Kinker had been one of my first-graders, but only Mr. Kinker survived. A few weeks after that storm, the bank in Cardinal foreclosed on their farm, and Mr. Kinker shot their horse and pig and then himself.

We'd never again use our storm cellar for protection. "Dust falls down, not up," Dad said when he announced his new plan. Our stairwell between the kitchen and parlor leading to bedrooms upstairs was enclosed, with a door at the bottom. Not completely safe, but the safest place we had. "A mountain of dust'd have to fall on us before we'd end up like those poor souls," he said. "Soon as a storm hits, get in the stairwell, everyone."

Lily didn't care about any plan. Not her. "If he really wants us safe, we should go to California," she'd said. But not so's Mom or Dad heard.

The Ardens' Model A appeared at the county road and kicked up billows of dust. Beezer, ever the great guard dog, ran over and yammered at the car wheels. As Opal slowed for Lily, the car lurched into our yard with sounds of grinding gears and Beezer's barks. Opal was a rotten driver, which was one of the reasons I didn't mind staying home, the other being I wasn't as partial to flirting with oil catters as they were. Most of those guys—ignorant rummies with missing teeth—weren't fit to flirt with.

Lily calmed Beezer and made him slink back to me. Then she jumped on the A's running board and pulled the door open. She gave me a salute and turned it into a wide wave. I couldn't hear her, but I saw clearly enough that she was giggling before she disappeared inside. I wished I could have giggled with her, but my gut told me nothing funny was going on. I watched the car turn around and leave, the tires kicking dust.

Beezer rubbed against my leg. The old fella knew when to give comfort. He followed as I trudged toward the chicken feed and egg basket set atop a barrel that stood beside a tall stand of bluestem. I scooped grain into the bowl, set it inside the basket and slipped my arm through the handles. Most of our hens died in the last dust storm, the same one that took the Kinkers. We had only four hens left. Wouldn't take me long to pluck eggs from four nests.

"Can't complain about losing chickens," Mom had said, "we still have each other." She had pressed a palm against her forehead. "All those years Brad and Molly Kinker spent building a family and a farm. All for nothing."

I had given her an energetic hug, but the feel of her shoulder blades—brittle bones with a thin layer of skin—had shocked me. I avoided strong hugs after that.

Crows screeched, and air jumped at me like attacking locusts. Grit flew in my eyes from all directions. I clutched the bandana with one hand and, with my free arm, I swung the basket and uselessly struck out. The dust devils danced higher. A thick black line appeared at the horizon. How could Lily and Opal make the twenty miles to Hayward? They'd be smack inside that blackness. I was angry at the rising wind, angry at Lily, and crazy mad at myself for agreeing to help her, for not telling Mom what my sister was up to.

SELF PORTRAIT

ALYS MASEK

I am a woman in my forties discovering
that to get old is to become invisible. At times
  I welcome
the way a man's eyes slide over me without seeing.
Other times I resent this, because as Kim
  Addonizio wrote
God damn it, I was once a beautiful woman.

Too many nights I sleep lightly if at all, waking on
  the hour
to a hard beating heart. By six am, arms snake
  around me
and a voice crying *mommy* jolts me into awareness.
I gulp tea for the caffeine and sugar. Even so
  by midmorning,
I am mostly exhausted. Though I am seldom alone,
I am many times lonely.

Whispers of poems, lines and words slink
into my brain and slip out again, quick as minnows.
I still read, dive into books
as if I could escape into their pages.

Too often, I turn from my husband
to my daughter. I lay beside her in the dark
feel her breathe and know I will never love
with such fierce concentration, such ruthless tunnel
  vision again.

Before bed, my daughter and I read a book about
  far places
in the world. When we get to a picture of an island
in the middle of the ocean, she points to it
and says *mommy* because that is where I used to live.
On an island in the middle of the Pacific.
On a boat anchored in a blue green lagoon.

Curled up in the cockpit, drinking tea, wearing
a sundress splashed with hibiscus
trade winds rocking the boat, I dreamed of her.
In the salt, in the sun, in the clear water,
among the bright colored fish, the sea birds
darting and wheeling, I dreamed a daughter
  into being.

OLD FRIENDS

UNA NICHOLS HYNUM

We walk the perimeter of the pasture
where it meets the piney woods.
The heavy odor of cows hangs in the air.
Wearing a pair of Matthew C's boots
I'm in danger of walking out of them
as we squish across the sodden field
dodging cow flops, laughing.
The sky is pewter. Clouds stagger,
threatening a gusher of summer rain.
He wants to share this little corner of the Texas
he loves, bluebonnets, blue bells, primroses
and quinine weed, to taste wild huckleberries.
We've left our spouses back at the house.
If we are in love, it doesn't occur to us to say so.
a spider-silk shimmying
between the gate posts
He shows me a roadside stand where he leaves
produce from his vegetable garden
with a glass jar for payment.
Matthew C believes in the honor system.

to leave I must break
spider silk shimmying
between the gateposts

ABOUT THE EDITORS

Bonnie ZoBell (prose): Bonnie Zobell recently won first place in the 2015 Next Generation Indie Press Award in the Novella category for her linked 2014 collection with Press 53, *What Happened Here: a novella and stories.* Her fiction chapbook *The Whack-Job Girls* was published in March 2013. She's won a National Endowment for the Arts fellowship in fiction, the Capricorn Novel Award, and a PEN Syndicated Fiction Award. A finalist for the James Jones First Novel Contest and the Nelson Algren Award, she's received fellowships at The MacDowell Colony, the Corporation of Yaddo, Virginia Center for the Creative Arts, Dorland Mountain Arts Colony, Villa Montalvo, and the Helene Wurlitzer Foundation. She has an MFA from Columbia University, currently teaches at San Diego Mesa College and is working on a novel. Visit her at www.bonniezobell.com.

Sydney Brown (poetry): A graduate of San Diego State University's MFA program in Creative Writing, Sydney Brown is the Co-Coordinator of the Creative Writing Program and Director of the Fall Reading Series and Literary Arts Festival at Grossmont College, where she also teaches literature, creative nonfiction, and composition. In addition, she facilitated a popular poetry workshop at the college for eight years. Her writing has appeared in numerous literary journals, including, but not limited to, *Sunshine/Noir: Writing* *from San Diego and Tijuana, Inside English, Red, Two Girls Review, The Southern Anthology, Zaum: The Literary Review of Sonoma State, Angelflesh, San Diego Writer's Monthly, and How2: Contemporary Innovative Writing Practices by Women.* In 2010, she was a finalist for the Marsh Hawk Press Poetry Prize and a semifinalist for the Persea Books Poetry Prize.

CONTRIBUTORS

Claire Hsu Accomando graduated from NYU with a degree in biology but always preferred literature to science. Her poems were published in *Atlanta Review, California Quarterly, San Diego Reader, Mudfish, Perigee, San Diego Writers Ink, The San Diego Poetry Annual,* and in *Magee Park Poets Anthologies*. Her non-fiction works include *Love and Rutabaga* (St. Martin's Press), and publications in *Women in World History, The Christian Science Monitor, American History Magazine, Ararat, Artweek, Promising Practices,* and other magazines.

Diana Avery Amsden, Ph.D. (DianaAmsden.com) grew up near Santa Fe. Her background is mostly anthropology, archaeology, art history, and architecture. She worked in academia, the corporate world, and Hollywood, and designed adobe homes in New Mexico. She has written short stories, novellas, and novelettes. Her upcoming novel, *The Stained Glass Woman,* a trilogy, is a multigenerational family saga that follows identical twins reared apart. It is a study of the Old Order Amish mindset from inside, outside, and down the generations. Her male and female psychopaths escape police radar, ravaging and devastating lives via family abuse: parent child, child parent; husband wife, wife husband; sibling sibling. The drivers of her tale include money, medical malpractice, Harvard, and Ayn Rand.

Meghan Anderson graduated from UCSD with a degree in Visual Arts Media. Her love of films and books stems from her interest in good storytelling. She currently lives in Oceanside, CA. When Meghan's not working on video productions, she busies herself with writing short stories.

As a mentor with the International Rescue Committee, **Judy A. Bernstein** met co-authors, Benson Deng, Alephonsion Deng, and Benjamin Ajak. Deeply touched by their epic journey, and heroic survival, she co-authored *They Poured Fire on Us from the Sky: The True Story of Three Lost Boys of Sudan.*

Krisa Bruemmer's writing was featured in the First Annual SDWI Memoir Showcase and the Olfactory Memoirs Preview Performance at The Ink Spot. She is currently working on a book based on her childhood experiences growing up in a dysfunctional family on a small island in Washington State.

E. Jacobs Burroughs was raised and educated in the Midwest, but rooted in southern landscapes and cadences. An English teacher by passion and profession, she retired from teaching in 2006 from MiraCosta Community College. Nowadays, Evelyn pursues her second passion: writing poetry worth reading.

Allen Fraser Clark's poetry has appeared in *Assaracus, The Far East, Arts & Understanding, The San Diego Poetry Annual,* and online in The Good Men Project, and HIV Here & Now. His Vietnam memoir piece, "Redacted," was selected for inclusion in a special program by the Old Globe Theatre in San Diego.

Kaleb Cook has been writing poetry for over ten years. He has taken classes at Grossmont College under Ryan Griffith, Karl Sherlock, and Sydney Brown, and is a far better writer and thinker because of it. His work has been featured in *The Finger, Words Dance,* and the *Black Fox Literary Magazine.*

Carrie Danielson grew up in the Colorado Rockies. Her first career was acting but later became an English teacher. Now retired, she has time to devote to writing. Carrie lives in Chula Vista, is married, has four children, and spends time with her four grandchildren, four dogs, and a parrot.

Alephonsion Deng was seven years old when his village in Southern Sudan was attacked. He fled into the night without food, water, shoes, or parents, and he crossed a 1,000 miles of war torn territory. His memoir *They Poured Fire on Us From the Sky* has won many awards including the Christopher.

Leslie Ferguson is a freelance writing coach and former English teacher. She holds an MFA in Creative Writing from Chapman University. Her current projects include a collection of poetry and a novel based on events from her childhood. She lives in Southern California.

Janet Foster's poetry has appeared in *New Millennium Writings, Enhance Magazine, The San Diego Poetry Annual,* and on the *Bluestocking Books* website. She also has published articles and book reviews in the San Francisco Bay Guardian, The San Francisco Review of Books, and Furious Fictions, among other publications.

Mary J. Fry's first book, *Adobe Doorways,* won the Pegasus Award, Oklahoma Federation of Writers. Her screenplay, *Denim & da Vinci* has garnered serious Hollywood attention. She also has published in several literary publications—*The Brushfire Literary and Arts Magazine* and *A Year in Ink, Volume 8.*

Michelle Furtado grew up in Toronto, Canada with her family, who immigrated from Nairobi, Kenya, and Goa, India. Her current project, "A Friend in Mind," is a bittersweet coming of age story of an Indian girl with schizophrenia. Her short story "Black Beatle" will be featured in the upcoming premiere issue of *The Literary Vine Anthology of Short Stories.* Michelle studied at The University of Toronto, earning a B.A., B.Ed, and M.A.(T.E.). She lives in San Diego with her husband, two daughters, and dog. Find her at https://michelle-furtado-n1ph.squarespace.com

Sean Kevin Gabhann is a Vietnam-era combat veteran of the US Navy. He first became interested in American Civil War history during the centennial celebration, and he owns an extensive library of primary and secondary material related to Civil War. He especially wants to write about campaigns in the West because of a fascination with the careers of US Grant and W.T. Sherman. Gabhann lives in San Diego, California with his wife, four sons, two daughters-in-law, three grandsons, three dogs, and a cat named Pepper who sometimes thinks she's a dog.

Judy Geraci writes. Sometimes it works out okay. Sometimes she just recycles old pieces that haven't seen the light of day in years, because she's still fond of them. She thanks you for reading her work and hopes you enjoy it.

Joan Gerstein, a retired educator and psychotherapist, has been writing poetry since childhood. Originally from NY and living in CA since 1969, Joan brings her experiences from both coasts to her writing.

Estelle Gilson is a writer, translator, and poet. Her most recent volume of poetry is titled Ms. Juvenal. Her translation of Italian poet Umberto Saba's only novel, *Ernesto,* is forthcoming. She maintains a web page at www.estellegilson.com

Allie Gove lives in El Dorado Hills, CA and writes both poetry and fiction. She began writing fiction after being captivated at a young age by stories like *Harry Potter* and *The Lord of the Rings* and began writing poetry seriously for the first time in creative writing classes in community college. Her work has appeared in or is forthcoming from *The Fat City Review, Black Fox Literary Magazine, Words Dance, WTF??!,* and *Milkfist.*

Cheryl Heineman is in the MFA program at SDSU. She has a master's degree in Jungian Psychology and has self-published two collections of poetry. Her poems have appeared in the *San Diego Poetry Annual,* and she has won several awards from the Palm Springs Writers Guild.

Retired SDSU Premedical advisor, **Barbara Huntington**, is a gardener, photographer, and writer whose poems, prose, and/or photography have appeared in her blog (http://barbarahuntington.com), *A Year in Ink, San Diego Poetry Annual,* and in Zen and Tibetan Buddhist newsletters. She has gratefully attended workshops with Jane Hirshfield, Steve Kowit, Naomi Shihab Nye, and other respected teachers.

Una Nichols Hynum, a local poet, has been nominated for Pushcart 2015, *San Diego Annual* editor Bill Harding.

Anthony Jesse is a native San Diegan and a member of San Diego Writer's Ink. He is a conservatory trained classical guitarist and his non-fiction works have appeared in music-related publications. "Silence" is his first published creative work.

Marianne S. Johnson practices law in San Diego. Her poetry is published in several journals including *Calyx* and *New Millennium Writings,* and multiple anthologies, including *Lavanderia* and *Sunshine Noir II*. Her poetry chapbook, *Tender Collisions,* was published by Aldrich Press in 2015, and she has been nominated for a Pushcart Prize.

Denise Angelle Kinsley holds an MFA in Creative Writing from the Jack Kerouac School of Poetics at Naropa University. She wrote a book of poetry published in 2009 and has published several poems and short stories in literary magazines and journals Denise is currently working on a short story collection.

Nancy Lemke's love of poetry developed taking Steve Kowit's poetry classes at Southwestern College. She has written two books, *Juan Rodriguez Cabrillo* and *The Missions of Southern California,* and was on the staff of *ZOONOOZ*.

Multimedia, multidimensional creative artist **J Lonack**, brings to her creations a passion for reimagining everyday items, harmonizing opposites, playing with current beliefs and assumptions using a whimsical twist, brushstroke-imagery poetry, and delicately blending spontaneity with discipline. The end results are simple, balanced expressions of wonder and joy.

Alys Masek is a public interest attorney. She lives in San Diego, California with her husband and two daughters. Her work has previously appeared in *The Noe Valley Review, City Works, Tall Grass, Hunger and Thirst,* and *Knocking on the Door.*

Joseph Milosch graduated from San Diego State University. His poetry has appeared in various magazines. He has multiple nominations for the Pushcart and received the Hackney Award for Literature. His books are *The Lost Pilgrimage Poems* and *Landscape of a Hummingbird*.

Amy Nastase lives in Oceanside with her husband and toddler daughter. When she is not writing, she enjoys playdates in the park and library storytimes.

Suzana Norberg's memoir, *Too Lazy To Be Satan,* chronicles the tragicomic hijacking of her life when, at the age of 24, she recklessly married a middle-aged "born-again" Christian who turned out to be a modern day Elmer Gantry. Her agent is currently pitching the manuscript to New York publishers.

Claudia Poquoc, known among classroom children as Grandmother Spider of the Word Wise Web, is also a singer/songwriter. Her first book, *Becomes Her Vision,* is a poetry/songbook which includes a CD. *Keeper of the Fields,* published in October of 2014 is her first full-length poetry book featured at the San Diego Public Library's Local Authors Exhibit in January of 2016.

Tully S. Reed is a writer and web developer. Whether writing about family life, tinkering with a poem, or simply making stuff up, she vows to keep listening to those inner and outer voices with a gentle hand and a sturdy pen.

Laurie Richards writes, teaches, and practices law in North County. She enjoys delving into San Diego's vibrant writing community through workshops for the Osher Institute and the Pasadena Library One City/One Story event.

She spends time trying to figure out whether to write horror, mystery or literary, short stories, or novels.

Ron Salisbury is a writer living in San Diego where he continues to publish, write, and study in San Diego State University's Master of Fine Arts program, Creative Writing. Publications and awards include: *Serving House Journal, Spitball, Soundings East, The Briar Cliff Review, Hiram Poetry Review,* etc; Winner of Main Street Rag's 2015 Poetry Prize, *Miss Desert Inn* was published November 2015.

Ravinder Sangha was born in India and settled in San Diego, California with her husband and two teenage sons. She likes cooking for her family, hiking, looking for stories in people and things, taking photographs of ordinary objects from different angles, and listening to bird-songs and music.

David J. Schmidt has published books, short stories, and articles in English and Spanish. His books include *Holy Ghosts: True Tales from a Haunted Christian College,* a study of haunting phenomena, and *Más frío que la nieve: cuentos sobrenaturales de Rusia,* a collection of supernatural horror stories set in Russia. He splits his time between San Diego and Mexico City.

Sarah Z. Sleeper's poetry was published in *Painters & Poets* and exhibited at the Bellarmine Museum. Her fiction won recognition from *Writer's Digest*. She has an MFA, is an editor for New Rivers Press, and received a 2016 artist's residency at Ragdale. Past accomplishments include three journalism awards.

The past five years **Brian Thedell** (brianthedell.com) has published and re-published his poetry wordpress, haunted various local open mics, and instigated poetry generally. In addition to SDWI, his work has appeared in the *San Diego Poetry Annual,* and upender.org.

Marg Wafer is a poet and a physical therapist, amazed by language and movement. She writes about the messy web of family and relationships, finding small trinkets, and old secrets. Marg is fascinated with the outdoor world and finds endless strands of poetry there.

ABOUT SAN DIEGO WRITERS, INK

San Diego Writers, Ink, serves as a hub for the literary communty, promotes literature, provides artistic development for writers at all levels, and facilitates artistic collaboration. A 501(c)(3) nonprofit organization, SDWI offers classes, groups, workshops, readings, and other literary events at The Ink Spot and other locations throughout San Diego County.

San Diego Writers, Ink
www.SanDiegoWriters.org

The Ink Spot
2730 Historic Decatur Road, Suites 202 and 204
San Diego, CA 92106
(619) 696-0363

A Year in Ink, an anthology published each year by San Diego Writers, Ink, represents a sampling of our community's most brilliant work. Each volume includes shorts stories, novel and memoir excerpts, creative nonfiction, satire, flash fiction, poetry, and more. The authors are a diverse group of young and old, new writers and much-published veterans. Several have had work in previous anthologies, most have been published in other literary journals, and a few allow *A Year in Ink* the honor of showcasing their first publication.

Explore the complete *A Year in Ink* collection available at our website.

A Year in Ink, Volume 1 (2008), edited by Thomas Larson

A Year in Ink, Volume 2 (2009), edited by Sandra Alcosser and Arthur Salm

A Year in Ink, Volume 3 (2010), edited by Roger Aplon and Jennifer Silva Redmond

A Year in Ink, Volume 4 (2011), edited by Jericho Brown and Laurel Corona

A Year in Ink, Volume 5 (2012), edited by Brandon Cesmat and T. Greenwood

A Year in Ink, Volume 6 (2013), edited by Michael Klam and Anthony Bonds

A Year in Ink, Volume 7 (2014), edited by Shadab Zeest Hashmi and Jim Ruland

A Year in Ink, Volume 8 (2015), edited by reg e gains and Dean Nelson

A Year in Ink, Volume 9 (2016), edited by Bonnie ZoBell and Sydney Brown

www.ingramcontent.com/pod-product-compliance
Lightning Source LLC
Chambersburg PA
CBHW070926250626
47159CB00009B/3134